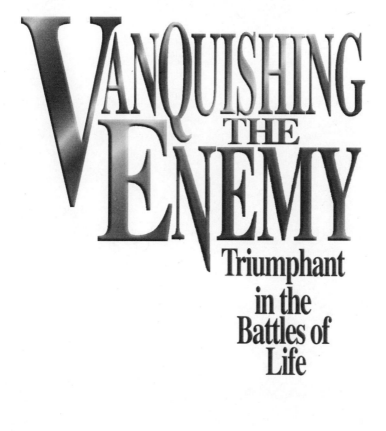

VANQUISHING THE ENEMY

Triumphant in the Battles of Life

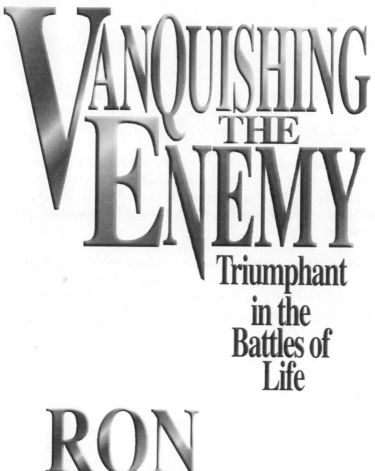

VANQUISHING THE ENEMY

Triumphant
in the
Battles of
Life

RON PHILLIPS

Pathway
PRESS
Cleveland, Tennessee

DEDICATION

Martin Luther, the Great Reformer, said, "Where the battle rages there the loyalty of the soldier is tested." Two loyal soldiers have borne with me the heat of spiritual warfare with courage and fealty. These are my colleagues:

Angie McGregor and Eddie Adams

Neither has wavered even in my most intense moments of spiritual battle. Eddie walked with me to the spiritual battlefield and has never left my side, no matter how tough the struggle. Angie rescued this project from oblivion because she knows, in her own soul, the victory that this book proclaims. You both have helped me "Vanquish the Enemy" in my own life. Indeed, in your own unique ways, you both have saved my life and ministry. I am forever thankful to you both for your friendship and love.

CONTENTS

PART ONE

THE BATTLE JOINED

1

THE ROAD TO RENEWAL

Some of the most miserable people I know are active professing Christians. As I sped westward toward Albuquerque, I knew I had become one of that tribe! For whatever accumulated reasons, after 10 years of a busy successful ministry I wanted to quit.

This was not normal ministerial wanderlust—a disease that affects the clergy, and whose symptoms are a mad belief that another place of service can fill the void of a lost spiritual relationship. No, this awful agony was a desire to leave the ministry.

Here I was flying at 600 miles per hour toward a speaking engagement, writing out my resignation from the ministry. Was this burnout? I had no idea that the living God had different plans. I was about to begin a journey to fullness.

I arrived the night before my scheduled morning speaking time, and was immediately frustrated by my room assignment. It was the only one on the hall— far away from the action. I checked the program to see who the other speakers would be. I knew the preacher scheduled to speak, but had never heard the woman on the program.

But it would be her message on prayer and knowing God that would utterly crush my proud heart.

The next day I sat in the back of the auditorium and listened to her story unfolding. The wife of a seminary professor who became a state executive, she was thrust into crisis by her husband's sudden death. He had been her spiritual resource and rock. In the back of an ambulance, she faced the reality that all of their shared life was abruptly ending. Now, she needed Jesus as never before; and He proved Himself faithful.

This message hammered at my self-pity and self-sufficiency. I believed right. I worked hard. I had read all the deeper-life books, yet I had lost the reality of God's presence. Joyless and worn out, God's Word hammered at my desire to go AWOL.

Struggling inside I made my way back to my room and collapsed on the bed, weeping. That night, out of a deep sleep I heard my name being called. Awakened, I went to the door and found no one. Soon I was sleeping again and was startled awake by hearing my name called a second time. The same thing had happened again. Like Samuel, I knew God had awakened me.

For me it proved to be a great awakening. I was led to pick up my copy of the Scriptures and turn to the reading for that day, Psalms 91–95. Graciously, God spoke to me out of that ancient account. God had not moved, I had! He was still in the secret place awaiting my fellowship. Further, He had "fresh oil" with which to anoint my stale spiritual life. That little room became a sanctuary, and the presence of Jesus swept over me.

In Psalm 91:1, 2 we read, "He who dwells in the secret place of the Most High shall abide under the shadow of the Almighty. I will say of the Lord, 'He is my refuge and my fortress; my God, in Him I will trust.'" I rediscovered the importance of a devotional life. I became aware that we are in spiritual warfare, facing infernal and invisible forces of wickedness. Prayer came alive in me again. "He shall call upon Me, and I will answer him; I will be with him in trouble; I will deliver him and honor him" (91:15).

Prayers poured forth from my aching heart—prayers of repentance, worship, and intercession. Through the night God visited me with a fresh filling of His Holy Spirit.

These scriptures came alive! God spoke to me through His precious Word. Here was the message I received that evening.

Psalm 92:10-15 challenged my heart to understand the fullness of the Holy Spirit. Verse 10 says, "I have been anointed with fresh oil." As I read the verses in that psalm, I could see what had been available to me all the time through the anointing of the Holy Spirit:

1. My eyes and ears would be open and perceptive to the things of God (v. 11).

2. My life could again flourish and grow (v. 12).

3. The house of God would again be a place I would enjoy (v. 13).

4. The aging process would have no effect on my spiritual life (v. 14).

5. My mouth would be open to praise the Lord for His goodness (v. 15).

After speaking later that day, I flew home thinking everything was going to be better! Little did I know that I had begun a hard journey with Jesus—a journey that contained dark valleys between the mountain-tops. I had no idea how desperately I would need the resources I had rediscovered.

The year ahead would be, in the words of Charles Dickens, "the best of times and the worst of times." The Spirit-filled life is not only a life of spiritual worship. The Enemy saw what God was beginning, and he unleashed a relentless attack on everything precious in my life.

2

ALL HELL BREAKS LOOSE

I heard of a boxer who was taking blow after blow. His manager kept hollering, "Stay with it, Joe, you are winning." After several rounds of this, Joe turned to his manager and said, "If I am winning, I wish somebody would tell *him*."

This is the way I felt as my life became a veritable battleground on all fronts for a two-year period. Depression lived at our house. When I returned from that life-changing encounter with the Lord, I found myself immediately in a struggle at home.

Difficulties at Home

In the fall of 1990, both my daughter and my wife totaled their cars on successive days. Heather, my daughter, was not seriously injured, and miraculously her car did not go into a flooded creek. She did, however, suffer a blow to the head that has created recurring difficulties including minor seizures.

My wife, Paulette, was nearly killed. I remember that September morning and the man on the telephone telling me Paulette had been in an accident not far from the house. I drove over the hill on Highway 153 and saw a terrifying scene before me.

Paulette was trapped for 45 minutes in her little Sunbird. All the bones on the left side of her upper body were broken or crushed. Even some of her teeth were cracked from the blow. She went into shock and nearly died, but the rescue team saved her life. For three months she had to have constant care.

In March 1991, my dad died suddenly. After struggling all his life with alcohol addiction, he was saved and ordained a deacon at the age of 59. We had become very close. On Sunday night before his death, he and I talked by phone for an hour. He was my great encourager. Now, at age 69, Dad was gone.

Trouble at Church

On the church front a woman committed suicide. Then her best friend was hospitalized in a mental unit. She threatened suicide unless I came immediately to see her. I and the associates went up to visit. When we sat down in the room, other voices poured forth from the woman. One of my associates, Eddie Adams, who is gifted in the area of prayer and spiritual warfare, began to identify and dismiss these cursing infernal enemies.

In less than an hour 13 demonic entities identified themselves as suicide, lust, death, cancer, depression, fear, rebellion, rejection, and others. All of them had English names; but as they were asked their real names, in the authority of Jesus, they would reveal their real natures only after a struggle. This dear lady is still recovering and needs counseling because of past wounds of the Enemy; but she is better, and I believe will be totally well in the future.

This experience opened my eyes to another world, another realm. Suddenly I realized that what had been theory was real warfare! Had I been, as a pastor, some kind of spiritual Don Quixote, fighting with windmills while my people were living in bondage?

I fell to my knees, and God's Spirit spoke gently to my spirit. He said, "This is what you asked Me for."

19

Yes, I wanted the reality of God, and I was discovering from my own pain and from the bondage of others a new direction and passion for ministry.

Immediately the Lord led me to invite a gifted minister friend to come and lead a spiritual-warfare conference. He was a longtime friend in whom God had brought renewal. He and I, along with others, prayed together for months for God to move in life-changing power.

In June 1991, this friend came and began to preach on "Strongholds in the Believer's Life." From the very first service God began to set people free. Revival came to the church and the meeting had to be extended. Literally hundreds of people had their lives changed during the meeting. Since that day we have seen hundreds more set free through prayer and spiritual warfare. Some of their stories will be found later in this book.

Some were not happy. Years before, through the ministry of Jack Taylor, God had revealed to me the truth of praise and worship. Later, in a worship seminar with Dr. Jack Hayford, God convicted me of my own lack of worship and taught me to worship and love Jesus publicly. As old forms, ideas, and traditions fall, some people grow uncomfortable. Surprisingly, a staff member came and accused me of frightening the people and of not being a true Baptist. Already the

Enemy had rallied a small group to try to kill the revival and renewal that had come.

At this point one of our secretaries, a member, lost her husband to a sudden heart attack. She was left with a teenage son and daughter. She was diagnosed with a bad heart and faced the possibility of life-threatening surgery. When I got the news, my wife and I went immediately to pray for her before she went into the hospital. The Holy Spirit spoke clearly to me and told me, "This [sickness] is not from Me and will not stand." I prayed over my friend, rebuking a spirit of infirmity and death. Miraculously, when they examined her the next day, all the symptoms were gone!

God was moving mightily in saving power and ministering power. Yet, an unrest and heaviness still seemed to be present at times. The opposing staff member appeared to grow distant, nervous, and uneasy around me. God was about to rip the scab off the church's most horrific problems.

In November 1991, this staff member was arrested for acts of pedophilia against five young men over a six-year period. He had served as a staff member at Central for 17 years! More than 1,500 young people had been a part of his ministry across the years. Only a handful knew about these alleged acts.

These accusations were not discovered because the boys came forward, but rather, in my opinion, by divine providence. A young man picked up a practice tape and found recorded on the opposite side an intimate conversation between this staff member and a 14-year-old boy. An investigation ensued and the police came to the church one Tuesday afternoon with a search warrant. I could not believe what my eyes saw when his briefcase was opened—hard-core pornography that he admitted purchasing for these boys' use.

Immediately we asked for, and received, his resignation. The next day he was arrested and the charges piled up, as more alleged victims were discovered by examining his cache of files, pictures, and tapes. The publicity around this situation whirled for months.

Personal Struggles

In the middle of these struggles, I was attacked with a life-threatening situation. One Thursday evening Kelli, my grown daughter, came over to spend the night because she had dreamed that I was sick. That night around 1:00 a.m., I awoke sick and dizzy. I went to the bathroom and collapsed there, losing consciousness. My daughter heard the fall in the other room and came in to see what it was.

In my unconscious state I was at peace. I caught a fleeting glimpse of the brightness and glory of another world, and for a moment I smelled the sweet atmosphere of the other world. Then, as if far away I could hear Kelli's voice calling, "Dad, Dad . . ." and I came back. I was hospitalized for a week with stress-related heart problems and still take a pill every day to keep the heartbeat steady.

It was this experience that taught me the key truth of spiritual warfare: the battle is not ours, but His. My heart doctor walked in to me and said, "Pastor, you must practice what you preach if you are going to live." Out of this time God taught me what I will be sharing with you in the rest of this book. God can equip you to do His work and will.

The former staff member's original trial was held in April 1992. Prior to the trial, some well-meaning but misinformed (in my opinion) people rallied at his house. This former staff member had privately promised me not to have contact with the young people and not to stir up trouble in the church. Nevertheless, there was soon an open conflict.

The former staff member was convicted and began to serve a term in prison.

I was caught between the people who rallied to this person, and the angry and hurt families of the victims. My wife and I saw people who had been our friends for years walk away from us. Yet, the church as a whole continued to pray, worship, and reach out. In fact, though 324 members left the church by letter during the two years following the incident, we added 700, including 310 baptisms. That was miraculous.

In July 1992, the church was sued for $10 million by these families who were our members at that time. The suit was settled through Biblical mediation. The church continued to grow spiritually and numerically in the midst of that storm. God met every need. We continue to seek God's face and pray for the victims and their families, that every genuine need will be met and healing will come.

Personally, this struggle has been painful for me. The accused staff member and I were friends, though I never had a hint of his secret life. As far as I am aware, the only ones who really knew were the alleged victims and this man. Though some of the families had questioned his special interest in certain youths—both male and female—no evidence was ever discovered prior to his arrest.

As this book goes to press, the media is reporting that the former staff member's convictions have been overturned on legal technicalities. They report that a new trial is scheduled.

When these horrible things happen, people want to blame others. The sad truth, I believe, is that this man was demonically directed and could deceive. In 2 Corinthians 11:13-15 the Scriptures say:

> For such are false apostles, deceitful workers, transforming themselves into apostles of Christ. And no wonder! For Satan himself transforms himself into an angel of light. Therefore it is no great thing if his ministers also transform themselves into ministers of righteousness, whose end will be according to their works.

You see, it is no big deal for Satan to counterfeit a minister. It is possible that our church could have lived in deception for years. Only when revival came did God finally expose evil. People would do well to realize that some things can't be blamed on others. We must see the Enemy for who he is and expose his works.

The material which follows is designed to equip you to do battle over the spiritual darkness that comes against you. The Christian walks through a war zone. Yet, the victory is ours. God rarely removes difficulty, but He walks us through these valleys. God is determined to teach us that we cannot live without Him. We need to be "fully furnished" with the spiritual armor and resources that are already ours.

3

EXPOSING THE EVIL EMPIRE

Finally, my brethren, be strong in the Lord, and in the power of His might (Ephesians 6:10).

A few years ago President Ronald Reagan referred to the former Soviet Union as "the evil empire." Like all evil empires of the past, the Soviet Union is gone. Yet, other nations have exploded in conflict and new empires of evil are arising.

The ultimate "empire of evil" is an unseen one. Sinister forces of unspeakable strength and terror lurk behind the chaotic, brutal, and inhumane actions on this planet. These forces are clearly identified and confronted in Scripture. They are called Satan, demons, principalities, powers, rulers of the darkness, spiritual forces of wickedness, fallen angels, and princes of darkness.

James S. Stewart was far ahead of his time when he focused on the demonic in the 1951 Yale lectures. He pointed out the reality of the Cross and its application as a death blow to these evil entities. Further, he saw the trend of many in psychology and psychiatry to deny the reality and personality of evil forces. The following are some of the warnings this Anglican scholar issued 40 years ago. In *A Faith to Proclaim,* a volume of the 1951 Lyman Beecher lectures, Dr. Stewart laments the loss of spiritual warfare. These excerpts are from the chapter "Proclaiming the Cross":

It was Gerald Heard who said: "Newton banished God from nature, Darwin banished Him from life, and now Freud has banished Him from His last stronghold, the soul." I wish to introduce the theme of Preaching the Cross by suggesting that, if for great numbers of our contemporaries the effort of Newton, Darwin and Freud has been to banish the divine, it has even more emphatically been to banish the demonic. St. Paul's "principalities and powers"—the "spirit forces of evil" whose malignant grip upon the souls of men called

forth "a second Adam to the fight and to the rescue"—
are now known, we are told, to have been mere apoc-
alyptic imagination.

To this result Newton, Darwin and Freud certainly
contributed. For Newton's work left no room for an
irrational principle in nature; and the devil is essentially irrational, teleologically indefinable—as St. John
marks by his significant use of *anomia* (1 John 3:4)
and St. Paul by the phrase "the mystery of iniquity"
(2 Thessalonians 2:7). "Only he who understands
that sin is inexplicable, knows what it is" (Brunner).
Again, Darwin's picture of the biological struggle for
existence was hailed as radically superseding the
Biblical picture of the cosmic struggle between the
demons and the kingdom of the Lord. Finally, Freud
banished the powers of darkness from their last
stronghold, the soul, by successfully dissolving them
into psychological complexes, neuroses, and the like:
so that the good fight of faith becomes simply a matter of inner individual adjustment. (James S. Stewart,
A Faith to Proclaim [New York: Charles Scribner's
Sons, 1953], pp. 76, 77).

Citing Reformation theologian John Calvin, Professor
Stewart continues:

We have lost the emphasis that what is really at issue
in the age-long tragic dilemma of Romans 7, what in
fact is always at stake in every moment of temptation,
is not a higher self or a lower self, personal integrity
or dishonor—that is the least of it: what is at stake is

the strengthening or (please God) the weakening of the spirit forces of evil that are out to destroy the kingdom of Christ. "For," says Calvin, "if the glory of God is dear to us, as it ought to be, we ought to struggle with all our might against him who aims at the extinction of that glory. If we are animated with proper zeal to maintain the kingdom of Christ, we must wage irreconcilable war with him who conspires its ruin." This is the insight which modern theological reconstructions have been apt to lose. We have lost Paul fighting with wild beasts at Ephesus and Luther flinging his ink-pot at the devil (pp. 78, 79).

He concludes this stirring chapter with a call to renewed passion and emotion in our cosmic struggle:

Were Paul to come back today and look upon the tragic conflict of our world, he would still say that "our wrestling is not against flesh and blood" (Ephesians 6:12), not against any group of men or nations, Caesarism or Communism, as though the interests of democracy were synonymous with the righteousness of God; it is nothing so simple and naive as that—God pity the facile imagination which assumes our own policies are blameless and our own hands clean. No, the real warfare cuts across all such alignments, and lies deeper down in the invisible realm where sinister forces stand flaming and fanatic against the rule of Christ. And the only way to meet that demonic mystic passion is with the *dunamis* and passion of the Lord. Was it not Christ's declared intention to kindle that flame in human hearts? "I am come to send fire on the earth" (Luke 12:49). For only Spirit can conquer spirit. The children of darkness are wiser in this than the children of light. The devil knows better than stifle emotion. And it is no use, in a day when spirit forces of passionate evil have been unleashed upon the earth and when fierce emotions are tearing the world apart, it is no use having a milk-and-water passionless theology: no good setting a tepid Christianity against a scorching paganism. The thrust of the demonic has to be met with the fire of the divine. As indeed it can: since Christ has overcome the world (pp. 102, 103).

The late Dr. Stewart's warning is now fulfilled prophecy. Our world is now captured by complexes, our children are victims of all sorts of mental maladies, and our culture needs pills to stay in control. As valuable as good psychology and psychiatry are, there is a sinister, evil army with which we struggle. Can we not live in the victory of Christ's cross today? My message is that we can live triumphantly in His victory.

On the contemporary scene M. Scott Peck, a noted psychologist and best-selling author, has written a book called *The People of the Lie.* Peck affirms that his own encounter with evil was not simply human activity, but it occurred in the realm of demonic activity.

Best-selling evangelical author Neil Anderson has effectively systematized and applied the truth of

31

spiritual freedom through his many works. His *7 Steps to Freedom* is indeed the best counseling method available to the pastor today. Anderson's book *The Bondage Breaker* effectively applies warfare truths to the individual. His book *Setting Your Church Free* applies the same truths to the institutional church.

This book is written to bring believers who are blind to the truth to a new awareness of their place in Biblical revelation. By reading again the Biblical basis for spiritual warfare, many will be moved to discover spiritual and personal freedom. Most Christians believe in Satan, yet are convinced that Christians cannot be affected by him. By simply ignoring or trivializing the truths of spiritual conflict, pastors and teachers often leave their people in bondage.

Not long ago in a large church I had the privilege of leading a young woman through Neil Anderson's seven steps to freedom. During the process the young woman exhibited some behaviors that included nausea, vomiting, weakness, and dizziness. The strongholds of hell in her life were broken and she was freed. Another woman observed the encounter and privately expressed outrage at me, attacking our team. She angrily threatened the pastor for allowing me to counsel the young woman. She herself was obviously demonized more than the young lady. She had a stronghold of deception and was blind to the spiritual reality she had observed.

The attitude of many in ministry is often, "Let the Charismatics do warfare; we don't need it." Spiritual warfare is disturbing to our Western sensitivities. We do not want to hear demons screaming at us. So we allow our people to live with tormenting strongholds from the past. We baptize them over and over because of old bondages. We refer them, drug them, and finally write them off.

We must fight the Enemy that comes against our flocks. I want to remind us of the militant Scriptures that call us to battle. This book is a wake-up call to all Christians. The Canaan of spiritual living must be dispossessed of its evil giants. We must march around the walls of the strongholds that hinder our possession of God's best—we must march until they fall!

4

THREE UNCHANGING FOUNDATIONS FOR SPIRITUAL WARFARE

You therefore must endure hardship as a good soldier of Jesus Christ. No one engaged in warfare entangles himself with the affairs of this life, that he may please him who enlisted him as a soldier. . . .

Be diligent to present yourself approved to God, a worker who does not need to be ashamed, rightly dividing the word of truth. But shun profane and idle babblings, for they will increase to more ungodliness. And their message will spread like cancer. Hymenaeus and Philetus are of this sort, who have strayed concerning the truth, saying that the resurrection is already past; and they overthrow the faith of some. Nevertheless the solid foundation of God stands, having this seal: "The Lord knows those who are His," and, "Let everyone who names the name of Christ depart from iniquity.". . .

And a servant of the Lord must not quarrel but be gentle to all, able to teach, patient, in humility correcting those who are in opposition, if God perhaps will grant them repentance, so that they may know the truth, and that they may come to their senses and escape the snare of the devil, having been taken captive by him to do his will (2 Timothy 2:3, 4, 15-19, 24-26).

Every Christian is a soldier at war (vv. 3, 4). If victory is to be enjoyed, the soldier's battle plan must rest on a solid foundation of sound teaching from the Word of God. The greatest snare of the Enemy is in the area of perverting or denying the truth.

God's foundations stand sure, and we must rest our faith, our planning, and our battle strategy on three unchanging Biblical and spiritual foundations: (1) the finished work of Christ, (2) the believer's union with Christ, and (3) the present work of the Spirit of Christ in the believer.

The Finished Work of Christ

All we have and are able to enjoy in the realm of the Spirit is based on the glorious fact that the Son of

God came in the flesh, invaded this demon-infested world, and wrought the victory through His death on the cross and resurrection from the dead.

Acts 10:38 says of Jesus, "How God anointed Jesus of Nazareth with the Holy Spirit and with power, who went about doing good and healing all who were oppressed by the devil, for God was with Him."

How did God win this victory? "They killed [Jesus] by hanging [Him] on a tree. Him God raised up the third day" (vv. 39, 40).

The late Professor James S. Stewart mourned the loss of teaching about the demonic powers and their defeat through the Cross. "[The] elimination of the dimension of the demonic has had its effect upon Christian theology," he stated (p. 77). He calls this loss "a usurping force, personal, alive, tyrannical" (p. 77). It is not simply some phobia of man or the divided self.

In His death Jesus did at least three things to assure our victory:

1. *He settled the sin question* (Romans 5:1-5; 8:1). Jesus Christ died as our sinless substitute. Once and for all He canceled our sin debt and Satan's right to accuse us.

2. *He came to make us acceptable in the Beloved* (Ephesians 1:6). Individually, we now have eternal significance.

3. *He came to conquer Satan* (Colossians 1:13; 2:15; Hebrews 2:14, 15; 1 John 3:8).

The atoning death of Christ was the battle of the ages. Unseen victories were being won. Theologian Gustav Aulen called Jesus' death and resurrection the dramatic theory of atonement and spoke of "the decisive irrevocable defeat of the powers of darkness" (p. 84). Christ's death was triumphant. P.T. Forsyth said: "The world's awful need is less than Christ's awful victory. And the devils we meet were fore-damned in the Satan He ruined. The wickedness of the world is, after all, 'a bull in a net,' a chained beast kicking himself to death" (*The Glorious Gospel*, p. 7).

John Calvin said, "There is no tribunal so magnificent, no throne so stately, no show of triumph so distinguished, no chariot so elevated as is the gibbet [cross] on which He has subdued death and the devil, and trodden them under His feet."

German theologian Oscar Cullman said of Christ's finished work that principalities and powers "between the Resurrection and the Parousia [Second Coming] are tied to a rope, still free enough to evince their demonic character, but nevertheless bound, since Christ has already conquered all demons: the Cross and the Resurrection being the decisive battle that has turned the tide of the war and settled the issue, even though Victory Day may still lie in a future out of sight.

We must always understand that we fight on the foundation of a victory already won!

Jesus came to cancel everything we inherited from the first Adam (Romans 5:12-21). In the Garden of Eden, Satan usurped the inheritance of humanity and enthroned death as the king of the earth. A "second Adam," Jesus Christ, was called forth to break the grip of these principalities and powers and to rescue the race from extinction (v. 17).

You and I must appropriate the finished work of Christ if we are to enjoy His victory. This brings us to the second foundation.

Our Union With Christ

The new birth (John 3:3) makes us alive by the Holy Spirit (Ephesians 2:1-9) and brings us into a vital union with Christ. Romans 5:10 says, "Having been reconciled, we shall be saved by His life." Indeed, His death for us secured our salvation; His life in us applies that salvation.

God changes our lives by *exchanging* our lives for the life of Christ. According to the New Testament we are now identified with Christ in every aspect of His finished work.

Our death with Christ. Galatians 2:20 says, "I have been crucified with Christ; it is no longer I who live, but Christ lives in me."

Our burial with Christ. Romans 6:4-6 declares that everything we were in Adam was buried with Christ. Baptism is a picture of that burial: "Therefore we were buried with Him through baptism into death. . . . Knowing this, that our old man was crucified with Him, that the body of sin might be done away with, that we should no longer be slaves of sin" (vv. 4, 6).

Our resurrection with Christ (Romans 6:4-6; Ephesians 2:1-6). Spiritually, the saved person has been raised out of spiritual death. Though our bodies have not been raised, the "resurrection factor" lives by the Holy Spirit in our spirit. In fact, the Holy Spirit is the "earnest" (KJV), or "guarantee," of our bodily resurrection (Ephesians 1:13, 14). Eternal life dwells in every believer.

Our enthronement with Christ. Ephesians 2:5, 6 says, "Even when we were dead in trespasses, [God] made us alive together with Christ (by grace you have been saved), and raised us up together, and made us sit together in the heavenly places in Christ Jesus").

When we look at Ephesians 1:20, 21, we see that when we take our position in Christ, when we are seated with Him, we are then "far above all principality and power and might and dominion." Everything that was once over our heads is now under our feet.

Our strategic position is identified fully with Christ. First John 4:17 says, "As He is, so are we in the world."

The Fullness and Power of the Holy Spirit

The blessed Holy Spirit, the third person of the Trinity, is Lord in the earth today (2 Corinthians 3:17). The Holy Spirit indwells every believer. He may be ignored, insulted, grieved, and quenched. However, He longs to fill, gift, and bring forth fruit in every believer.

The Holy Spirit alone turns the Word of God into a sword—the sword of the Spirit. "For the word of God is living and powerful, and sharper than any two-edged sword, piercing even to the division of soul and spirit, and of joints and marrow, and is a discerner of the thoughts and intents of the heart" (Hebrews 4:12). This sword is a part of our spiritual armor: "And take the helmet of salvation, and the sword of the Spirit, which is the word of God" (Ephesians 6:17).

The Holy Spirit alone makes effective praying possible. "Likewise the Spirit also helps in our weaknesses. For we do not know what we should pray for as we ought, but the Spirit Himself makes intercession for us with groanings which cannot be uttered" (Romans 8:26). We are admonished, "But you, beloved, building

41

yourselves up on your most holy faith, praying in the Holy Spirit" (Jude 20).

The Holy Spirit alone gives understanding of the Word of God. Ephesians 1:15-18 speaks of the gift of wisdom and revelation by the Holy Spirit. God's Spirit makes it possible to understand and apply spiritual truth.

The Holy Spirit strengthens our inner man. "That He would grant you . . . to be strengthened with might through His Spirit in the inner man" (Ephesians 3:16).

The Holy Spirit desires to fill every Christian. Ephesians 5:18 says, "Be filled with the Spirit." This fullness is no less than total control of the individual. This is the lordship of Christ active in the life of a Christian. A Spirit-filled believer cannot be defeated by Satan and his demonic forces. Filled with the Spirit we live in a constant state of triumph.

5

---

12 DANGEROUS MISCONCEPTIONS ABOUT SPIRITUAL WARFARE

Now the Spirit expressly says that in latter times some will depart from the faith, giving heed to deceiving spirits and doctrines of demons (1 Timothy 4:1).

The last days will be characterized by a departure from the faith. Included in this apostasy will be those deceived by seducing spirits and doctrines of demons. First Corinthians 10:20 warns about religion without Christ, and calls it a "sacrifice to demons." Second Corinthians 11:13-15 warns us of counterfeit ministries. Ephesians 6:11 challenges us all to "put on the whole armor of God." Today, many Christians are deceived to the point that they do not believe in the power of Satan and the awful influence of the demonic.

First Timothy 1:18 calls us to "wage the good warfare."

First Timothy 6:12 calls us to "fight the good fight of faith."

Too many Christians have ignored the Enemy and allowed him free reign in their lives. Some dangerous misconceptions about spiritual warfare need to be cleared up.

Misconception #1: Demons, Active in the Time of Christ, Are Active Today Only in Pagan Cultures

Nothing in the Bible restricts demonic operation to a certain time or culture. To the contrary, all Scripture speaks of the constant battle that is ours. We are warned to be constantly alert, "lest Satan should take advantage of us; for we are not ignorant of his devices" (2 Corinthians 2:11). One of his devices is to lead people to deny his existence.

Misconception #2: Demons Cannot Bother Believers

There is much debate over the use of the term "demon possession." In the New Testament, *demonization* is never used for a believer. No Christian can be totally taken over by demons, but every Christian can be oppressed, harassed, and dominated by the Enemy's activity.

In Acts 5:3, Ananias had his heart filled by Satan, and he lied to the Holy Spirit! Unrepentant believers can be turned over to Satan for the destruction of the flesh (1 Corinthians 5:4, 5). Paul said we are to wrestle against the powers of darkness, quench the Enemy's fiery spears, and stand firm against his assaults (see Ephesians 6:10-16). The Enemy can attack the mind and body of a Christian. Christians need to embrace deliverance as a part of their salvation.

The Lord's Prayer in Matthew 6:13 tells us to pray daily, "Deliver us from the evil one."

Misconception #3: Only Occult Involvement Leads to Demonic Difficulties

Occult involvement leads to demonization. However, occult involvement is not the only avenue to oppression by the Enemy. Every believer is subject to temptation, deception, oppression, and strongholds.

Misconception #4: Demonic Operation Incites Only Extreme Behavior, Such as Violence and Gross Sin

It is true, as seen in Mark 5, that total demonization can lead to extreme behaviors. Consider Mark 1:23, 24, however. A man in the synagogue cried out in his oppression. There was no violence there at all.

In Luke 13:10-16, a woman called "a daughter of Abraham" was bound by "a spirit of infirmity." Infirmity is *astheneia* in Greek; it means "feebleness, without strength, weakness." Jesus said to her, "You are loosed." The word *loosed* is *apoluo*, which means "to free fully and set at liberty." This woman had been sick and helpless because of demonic oppression for 18 years. She was a churchgoing believer, but bound by Satan for 18 years. Jesus set her free on the day of worship!

Misconception #5: Christians Are in Personal Danger When Dealing With Demons

I often hear people say in fear, "I do not want to stir up anything by getting involved in warfare." My friend, Jesus laid hands on this poor woman and she was delivered. Demons are under the authority of believers and can only affect us if we give them place.

What kind of surgeon would refuse to operate because of the fear of inflicting pain? What kind of doctor would refuse to treat a disease for fear of exposing himself. The doctor would protect himself and do his job. Likewise, we can suit up—be clothed with God's armor (Ephesians 6:10-17), and help others to freedom.

Misconception #6: It Is Dangerous to Touch or Be Around Others Who Are Demonically Afflicted

Fear invites the attack of the Enemy. However, other believers are not transmitters. A person who is right with God has nothing to fear from the Enemy.

Misconception #7: For Deliverance, We Can Just Plead the Blood of Jesus Without Understanding and Faith

The precious blood of Jesus is not some good-luck charm! We honor the blood of Jesus and trust its cleansing protection and delivering power. The blood pleads itself when applied to the life of the believer. Revelation 12:11 tells of the blood's overcoming power against Satan. The blood speaks of forgiveness and cancels the Enemy's right to attack. The blood does not "plead to Satan" for anything. The blood's plea is to the Father. The blood rebukes Satan! The song says:

> Let the blood of Calvary
> > Speak for me
> May it mark me down as righteous
> > Where no righteousness has been
> Free me from guilt and judgment
> > As it pardons all my sin.
>
> —Anonymous

Misconception #8: Instruction in Spiritual Warfare Is Unnecessary

Recently a pastor and a former long-standing member of the church I pastor informed me that the church had gotten along without this teaching for years. I replied, "Look at your church and mine." Half of our membership does not darken the door of the church. Sin is rampant. Depression and oppression dominates many of our people's lives. Ignoring the truth leads to disaster. Second Corinthians 2:11 warns us not to be "ignorant of [Satan's] devices."

Misconception #9: One Can Make Light of Satan and the Reality of Spiritual Warfare Without Impunity

An evangelist told me that Satan is a toothless tiger! That cliche sounds good, but is it true? The Bible says, "Be sober, be vigilant; because your adversary the devil walks about like a roaring lion, seeking whom he may devour. Resist him, steadfast in the faith" (1 Peter 5:8, 9). The word *devour* means "to gulp down." We must realize our Enemy is defeated but still dangerous.

Misconception #10: It Is Enough Just to Resist the Devil Over a Period of Time

Resisting the devil is necessary and important.

Yet this is defensive. There is an offensive side to spiritual warfare whereby ground gained by the Enemy must be retaken. In Matthew 12:43 demons seek "places." The same word is used in Ephesians 4:27: "Nor give place to the devil"! We must come to the rescue of those captured by the Enemy. In Colossians 1:13, those possessing salvation are "delivered . . . from the power of darkness." Jesus said of the church that "the gates of Hades shall not prevail against it" (Matthew 16:18). The church is to attack the very gates of hell's strongholds.

In John 12:31 Jesus spoke of the Cross as the place where the Enemy would be "cast out." Every lost person lives under the domain of "the prince of the power of the air, the spirit who now works in the sons of disobedience" (Ephesians 2:2).

When Paul stood before King Agrippa, he stated his mission: "To open their [the Gentiles'] eyes, in order to turn them from darkness to light, and from the power of Satan to God, that they may receive forgiveness of sins and an inheritance" (Acts 26:18). Salvation is a rescue of those in darkness under the rule of Satan.

Misconception #11: Freedom From Multiple Attacks of the Enemy Is Instantaneous

Sometimes it takes intensive warfare to get rid of all the invaders in your life. Years after his entry into the ministry, Timothy battled a stronghold of fear (see 2 Timothy 1:7). God will do a complete work if we let Him.

Misconception #12: Freedom in Christ Is the End of Spiritual Warfare

No, it is only the beginning of a life of discipleship. Ground retaken in one's life must be defended. Sin must be purged, and a life of commitment continued. We must wear our armor until that day we exchange it for a robe of white!

PART TWO

THE ENEMY UNMASKED

6

DISCOVERING CALVARY'S CONQUEST

As you therefore have received Christ Jesus the Lord, so walk in Him, rooted and built up in Him and established in the faith, as you have been taught, abounding in it with thanksgiving.

Beware lest anyone cheat you through philosophy and empty deceit, according to the tradition of men, according to the basic principles of the world, and not according to Christ. For in Him dwells all the fullness of the Godhead bodily; and you are complete in Him, who is the head of all principality and power.

In Him you were also circumcised with the circumcision made without hands, by putting off the body of the sins of the flesh, by the circumcision of Christ, buried with Him in baptism, in which you also were raised with Him through faith in the working of God, who raised Him from the dead. And you, being dead in your trespasses and the uncircumcision of your flesh, He has made alive together with Him, having forgiven you all trespasses, having wiped out the handwriting of requirements that was against us, which was contrary to us. And He has taken it out of the way, having nailed it to the cross. Having disarmed principalities and powers, He made a public spectacle of them, triumphing over them in it (Colossians 2:6-15).

A Biblical understanding of spiritual warfare begins at the end and not at the beginning. The reason for this is that it is ever important to keep our focus on Christ and not on the power of the Enemy. Satan has no rightful authority over any believer. He is a usurper and a trespasser on God's earth. We cannot even acquiesce to his proud claim to the kingdom of this world. This would be treason to the Christ who refused to avoid the cross by bowing to the Enemy in the wilderness temptation.

To go right to the heart of spiritual warfare, the battle has already been won! Satan has been under judgment since Eden. We must never forget that judgment was announced in Eden and implemented on Calvary! "And I will put enmity between you and the woman, and between your seed and her Seed; He shall bruise your head, and you shall bruise His heel" (Genesis 3:15). We must proclaim that the sentence handed down upon Satan in Eden has been executed.

Strong man that he is, Satan has been dispossessed by One stronger.

In John Bunyan's classic *Pilgrim's Progress*, when Timorous and Mistrust turned back from their journey to God's city, they saw two lions. "The lions were chained but they saw not their chains." Satan and the forces of hell are on a short leash since Calvary. We are not fighting for victory; we are fighting from victory. The bottom line of spiritual warfare is applying and enforcing the victory of the Cross on the Enemy. We cannot overestimate him, neither can we underestimate him.

We are not dualists who believe that God and the devil are equal and struggling for control of man. Satan does not coexist with God. The powers of darkness were conquered at the Cross. This tremendous passage in Colossians 2 reaches its climax in verse 15 with a victorious affirmation of Christ's victory: "Having disarmed principalities and powers, He made a public spectacle of them, triumphing over them in it."

Most of us see in the Cross the sacrifice of Christ for our forgiveness. We see the ultimate example of unconditional love. We see the demonstration of God's love to us. All this is certainly true, but there is a truth about what took place on the cross that some do not see: A cosmic spiritual war was waged that day.

Calvary was the culmination of all of Satan's hatred of Jesus. Satan tried to kill Jesus at His birth, using the tyrant Herod. He tempted Jesus in the wilderness to stray from the Father's plan. He set before the Lord the lust of the flesh, the lust of the eye, and the pride of life. He tempted Jesus' body, soul, and spirit. Jesus defeated Satan with the Word of God.

We should make no mistake about what the clear purpose of Jesus was in coming to the world: He came to do battle with Satan. The Lord Jesus Christ left heaven and invaded Satan's sphere. He came unwelcomed by the masses and was hated by Satan. In Jesus' inaugural address at the synagogue of Nazareth, He quoted Isaiah 61:1, 2: "The Spirit of the Lord is upon Me, because He has anointed Me to preach the gospel to the poor; He has sent Me to heal the brokenhearted, to proclaim liberty to the captives and recovery of sight to the blind, to set at liberty those who are oppressed; to proclaim the acceptable year of the Lord" (Luke 4:18, 19).

Jesus saw our world as bound, blind, brokenhearted, and bruised. He saw the disastrous effects of Satan's control. Throughout His ministry He confronted the forces of hell and cast them out. Many times He opened the eyes of the blind.

He still opens the eyes of those blinded by Satan. He still sets the captive free. Jesus saw the destructive work of Satan and did something about it.

The Bible is replete with verses that reveal these truths. In one of the many statements given about the purpose of the Lord's coming into the world, John tells us: "For this purpose the Son of God was manifested, that He might destroy the works of the devil" (1 John 3:8).

Shortly before the Cross, Jesus said, "Now is the judgment of this world; now the ruler of this world will be cast out" (John 12:31). When arrested, Jesus said to the soldiers, "When I was with you daily in the temple, you did not try to seize Me. But this is your hour, and the power of darkness" (Luke 22:53). The world in which He ministered was a world dominated by Satan. "We know that we are of God, and the whole world lies under the sway of the wicked one" (1 John 5:19).

Again, His purpose is stated by the writer of Hebrews: "Inasmuch then as the children have partaken of flesh and blood, He Himself likewise shared in the same, that through death He might destroy him who had the power of death, that is, the devil" (2:14).

The apostle Paul had no room for doubt about what took place in the spiritual realm on the day Jesus was crucified. In specific detail, Colossians 2:6-15 gives us a spiritual picture of the cosmic war that raged on Calvary that day. It also demonstrates to us our victory. Paul said three main things happened at the Cross that the natural eye could not see.

The Cross Disarmed Satan

Hostile spiritual powers had reigned over man and the world. This reign had its origin in sin and the Fall. Now Jesus had come to "spoil" (KJV) them. "Having disarmed principalities and powers, He made a public spectacle of them, triumphing over them in it" (Colossians 2:15).

The Greek word for *disarmed* means "to strip, or to rob." It is in the aorist tense in the Greek, which means it was a once-and-for-all disarming. There will not be a rematch—the battle has forever been decided. The word picture is that of a fallen enemy that has been stripped of his sword, armor, shield, position, and wealth. Scripture teaches us that Satan has been stripped of his right, power, and authority over all those who have bowed at the foot of the Cross and have received the precious blood of Christ as atonement for their sin.

What did Jesus rob Satan of? He robbed him of the right to accuse us: "Who shall bring a charge against God's elect? It is God who justifies. Who is he who condemns? It is Christ who died, and furthermore is also risen, who is even at the right hand of God, who also makes intercession for us" (Romans 8:33, 34).

Satan has been robbed of his right to kill us. We are no longer guilty. He has been robbed of his ownership of us. He has no weapon and no way to keep us.

The Cross Displayed Satan

Christ made a "public spectacle of them." Someone might object to this passage and say, "Wasn't it Christ who was made a public spectacle that day?" Indeed He was. He was stripped of His garments and made a public spectacle before men who cried, "If You are really God, then come down off the cross." But we must remember there was another public spectacle going on in the unseen spiritual realm.

In the spiritual realm Christ made a public spectacle of Satan and all of the demonic forces. Jesus displayed Satan before the angelic world, the demonic world, the spiritual world, and before "just men made perfect" (Hebrews 12:23). They saw him not as "an angel of light" as he so often would make himself appear, but rather they saw his true nature. They saw him as a rotten, filthy, lying thief. Satan and all of the demonic forces were viewed in their true nature.

Satan and all of his host flurried themselves in full fury against the seemingly helpless Son of God.

Satan came as "Apollyon," the destroyer (see Revelation 9:11). When the smoke of the battle lifted, there was an empty cross and an empty tomb. Jesus had defeated Satan on Satan's home field. This enemy was put on display as the defeated foe he really is. The word picture compares to a billboard. Satan was put on display for everyone to see.

Satan is forever a public spectacle of defeat when God's people enforce Calvary's victory. At His ascension Jesus passed through the atmosphere, declaring that neither the laws of gravity nor the powers of hell could hold Him back.

The Cross Defeated Satan

Dr. James S. Stewart, Scottish preacher and former chaplain to the Queen of England, was not popular when he stood for the fundamentals of the faith and called for a return to the truth "that a cosmic battle took place at the Cross." Behind the Cross we see the fallen design of man. Human sins such as pride, jealousy, greed, self-righteousness, religion, political injustice, and human apathy brought our Savior to the cross. Yet, behind these stood principalities and powers of evil. The people were driven by forces beyond themselves.

Jesus chose to die for His people because He knew the Enemy, as a strong man, had a death grip on them. He came as One stronger to set the captive free. Jesus acted in history not only to reconcile sinners but to expose the error of dualism. People everywhere feared the gods of superstition. Jesus not only defeated them, but the New Testament announced that they would bow before Him as Lord:

> Therefore God also has highly exalted Him and given Him the name which is above every name, that at the name of Jesus every knee should bow, of those in heaven, and of those on earth, and of those under the earth, and that every tongue should confess that Jesus Christ is Lord, to the glory of God the Father (Philippians 2:9-11).

The power of Satan was shattered at the Cross. Triumph over Satan had come at last. The verb *triumph* in Colossians 2:15 means a complete and irretrievable subjugation. The question remains, "If Satan has been disarmed, displayed, and defeated at the Cross, then why is my life so far from victorious?"

First, if you have not been saved, then you are fair game for the attacks and residency of Satan in your life. You cannot have victory over Satan apart from the application of the blood of Jesus to your sins.

Second, if you are a believer, then the only way Satan can attack you is if you have given him the right. "[Do not] give place to the devil" (Ephesians 4:27). If you have given place to the devil by living in rebellious sin, then you have put out a welcome mat for the Enemy to come and enslave you. Many believers live such defeated, depressed lives that they neither bring honor to the Lord nor set an example to others. These believers make up a weak, anemic church that is a blight to what Jesus accomplished on the cross. Jesus did not die for a church full of diseased, depressed Christians in bondage to the Enemy. He wants His people to be victorious.

There is victory in the Cross! The blood wiped out our sin and left Satan powerless. Every blow that drove the nails into His holy hands was also driving a nail in the coffin of Satan. Every Christian is set free. Christ's death was a battle in which God achieved an immortal victory. The conflict was furious and mysterious. Our Lord died to win the battle and rose from the dead to enforce the victory.

There is victory in Jesus every day. When Satan comes, we simply remind him of our Savior. If he accuses us, we point to forgiveness. If he desires to tempt us, we let our Lord's Word conquer him. If he would touch us, we declare that he has no authority over God's property.

7

OUR ANCIENT FOE

Moreover the word of the Lord came to me saying, "Son of man, take up a lamentation for the king of Tyre, and say to him, 'Thus says the Lord God:

"'You were the seal of perfection, full of wisdom and perfect in beauty. You were in Eden, the garden of God; every precious stone was your covering: the sardius, topaz, and diamond, beryl, onyx, and jasper, sapphire, turquoise, and emerald with gold. The workmanship of your timbrels and pipes was prepared for you on the day you were created.

"'You were the anointed cherub who covers; I established you; you were on the holy mountain of God; you walked back and forth in the midst of fiery stones. You were perfect in your ways from the day you were created, till iniquity was found in you.

"'By the abundance of your trading you became filled with violence within, and you sinned; therefore I cast you as a profane thing out of the mountain of God; and I destroyed you, O covering cherub, from the midst of the fiery stones.

"'Your heart was lifted up because of your beauty; you corrupted your wisdom for the sake of your splendor; I cast you to the ground, I laid you before kings, that they might gaze at you'" (Ezekiel 28:11-17).

Our own Western culture is the only society, both historical and contemporary, that has largely rejected the idea of evil spirits. Since the Age of Enlightenment the Western scholar has sought to understand the world through verifiable, rationalistic, and explainable terms. There is no place for good or evil spirit beings in this "scientific" era. While there is much good that has come from the scientific method, science has a large blind spot when it comes to the spiritual side of man.

Christians have no choice but to face the Scriptural, historical, and even contemporary fact that there is a supernatural enemy. Because of ludicrous literature and movies, the idea of a being who is supremely evil is viewed by many as a joke. Satan is caricatured as a red-suited villain with a tail, horns, and pitchfork. This is a serious underestimation of the Enemy.

Sun Tzu, the ancient Chinese philosopher, wrote *The Art of War* nearly 2,500 years ago. This book has become a classic on how to achieve victory in the battlefield. He said this about the enemy: "If you know the enemy and know yourself, you need not fear the result of a hundred battles. If you know yourself but not the enemy, for every victory gained you will also suffer a defeat. If you know neither the enemy nor yourself, you will succumb in every battle."

This is true in spiritual warfare. We must have a healthy recognition and knowledge of our Enemy, combined with a thorough knowledge of our own identity.

A contemporary story illustrates this truth. In January 1994, the Dallas Cowboy professional football team was preparing to play the San Francisco 49ers. Jimmie Johnson, coach of the Cowboys, caused a media uproar when he boldly asserted that his team would win on Sunday. He was questioned as to why he would make such a bold statement before playing such a talented opponent. His response was simple:

"I don't care who we are playing. I have seen my team in preparation this week. The fire is in their eyes. I don't have to measure the opponent, my team is ready." The Cowboys won.

In a similar fashion the Christian must balance the fierceness of the Enemy with the powerful resources on our side of this spiritual battle. When this is done we will exclaim with the prophet Elisha of old, "Do not fear, for those who are with us are more than those who are with them" (2 Kings 6:16).

Satan is a defeated foe because of the work of Christ on the cross, but he is also a formidable foe. Our struggle with him may be likened to the famous Battle of New Orleans in the War of 1812. General Andrew Jackson commanded the greatest battle of the war after the papers of surrender had been signed! Word had not reached them of the British surrender. We too fight in a battle that has already been decided. Jesus sealed the fate of the host of demonic forces, along with Satan himself forever, when He died on the cross. Yet Satan still "walks about like a roaring lion, seeking whom he may devour" (1 Peter 5:8). We must return to the Scriptures and see what God says about our Enemy.

The Formation of Satan

Surprisingly, the Bible does not give us a clear explanation of the origin of Satan. He is mentioned by name in only three texts of the Old Testament:

1 Chronicles 21:1; Job 1–2; and Zechariah 3:1, 2. His existence and nature are taken for granted; he is recognized as the spiritual being who opposes God, His purposes, and His people. Obviously the serpent in the Garden of Eden (Genesis 3) is assumed to be Satan. Here he appears without an explanation of his beginning.

Two passages of Scripture come later through the divine inspiration of the prophets, and they give us insight into this diabolical being's formation. They are Isaiah 14:12-15 and Ezekiel 28:11-17.

In the Isaiah passage, the prophet was predicting the fall of the king of Babylon when he began to describe the fall of a being who was obviously more than an earthly king. Here he is called "Lucifer," or "Day Star." Pride is revealed as the sin that led to his downfall. According to this passage he wanted to take the place of God. This certainly fits with the history of Satan's actions from the Garden of Eden to the wilderness temptations of Jesus. Satan's final judgment, according to Isaiah, is to be brought down to Sheol with the mockeries of those he terrified during his evil reign.

The passage in Ezekiel is far more informative. Like Isaiah, Ezekiel was predicting the fall of earthly kings. In chapter 28, Ezekiel proclaimed judgment against the kings of Tyre and Sidon. In verses 11-17, Ezekiel also moved beyond an earthly king's description in his prophecy.

Here are some of the reasons many view Ezekiel as talking about Satan in this passage:

First, there is no historical proof, or even reference, that Tyre ever had a king. During this period a prince ruled over Tyre, and he was overthrown (see vv. 1-10). A "king of Tyre" would be the father of this prince.

Second, verse 13 says to this king: "You were in Eden, the garden of God." According to Genesis 3, the only ones in the Garden of Eden were God, Adam and Eve, and the serpent. Since it is obvious that none of these other personages are being described, we feel confident, along with many other interpreters, that this is a symbolical reference to Satan.

Verse 13 also says this being was created. This reference gives us the opportunity to answer one of the often-asked questions, "Did God create evil?" If this passage is indeed a description of the formation of Satan, then we can answer resoundingly, "No!" Verse 15 refers to his creation: "You were perfect in your ways from the day you were created, till iniquity was found in you."

According to this, our spiritual enemy was created perfect, but with a choice which he one day exercised toward evil. God gave the angelic host a will to choose just as He did to man. This gives an accurate picture of the formation of Satan, but we must turn to a further description we find of him in the Bible.

The Features of Satan

According to Isaiah 14:12, Satan was originally called Lucifer, which means "light-bearer." In his pre-fallen state he was the highest of all the hosts of God. According to these descriptions he was beautiful to look upon and beautiful to listen to. Ezekiel 28:13 tells us that he was a veritable rainbow of iridescent colors. He was the combined brilliance of every precious stone. He was as valuable as the most costly stones and as beautiful as the colors of the rainbow. The problem was that stones do not give off light of themselves; they only reflect light. Satan evidently forgot this most important truth and became puffed up with pride.

He was also gifted musically. He was the very instrument of heaven. The ultimate purpose of music was to give highest expression to the praise of God. We see today how the Enemy uses music as one of his most effective tools to corrupt people in their thinking of God. The first mention of instruments in the Bible (except this pre-Creation example) is found in Genesis 4:21, where Jubal, one of Cain's descendants, is said to be "the father of all those who play the harp and flute."

This description is a far cry from what one would be led to believe by many people today. Paul warned in 2 Corinthians 11:14 that Satan can transform himself into an angel of light.

The Function of Satan

In his pre-fallen condition, the Enemy functioned around the throne of God. He was created as a cherub. This angelic being was created to guard the glory and holiness of God. Ezekiel 28:14 gives us this truth: "You were the anointed cherub who covers; I established you; you were on the holy mountain of God; you walked back and forth in the midst of fiery stones."

Cherubim were placed in the Garden of Eden to guard the Tree of Life after the fall of Adam and Eve (Genesis 3:24). Later, the ark of the covenant was to have replicas of two cherubim to overshadow the mercy seat.

The designation that Satan was the "anointed" cherub could mean that he was the head of the angelic host. This picture paints him as one who was beautiful and talented, one who was holding a very high rank (if not the highest), and one who was close to God. But all of this was not enough for him.

The Fall of Satan

In order to understand Satan's fall as the Scripture presents it, we must answer two vital questions: When did he fall? And why did he fall?

Many see the time of his fall as coming between Genesis 1:1 and 1:2. The scope of this book will not allow a lengthy defense of this cosmological view, but several key reasons need to be given because they bear on our understanding of the origin and function of the Enemy.

First, there is scriptural indication that God did not create the earth "without form, and void" originally. This evidence in Genesis 1:2 is found in the Hebrew words *tohuw* and *bohuw.* Isaiah 45:18 gives this description: "For thus says the Lord, who created the heavens, who is God, who formed the earth and made it, who has established it, who did not create it in vain, who formed it to be inhabited."

The word translated "vain" is the same Hebrew word, *tohuw,* translated in Genesis 1:2 as "without form." If God did not create the earth this way, then a catastrophe of cataclysmic proportions must have happened between these two verses. Genesis 1:3 and following seems to indicate a "re-creation" after an undesignated period of time. This is textually possible because the word *create* is *bara* in verse 1, which stands out to mean "to create something from nothing." Other words for *create* (excluding animal life) mean "to create out of existing materials."

Second, this would give us an understanding of many other scriptures. Jesus said in Luke 10:18, "I saw Satan fall like lightning from heaven." While many interpret this verse in light of the work of the Seventy whom Jesus had sent out, there is also strong merit to understand Jesus' statement in light of His pre-incarnate existence. This would help explain why the Enemy in the form of the serpent was already present in the Garden of Eden. The whole idea of Satan as a created angel that rebelled and fell along with other rebellious angels fits with this understanding of Biblical cosmogony.

A discussion of why the Enemy fell from heaven must follow. Isaiah 14:12-15 lists the steps that led to the Enemy's downfall. Five times in this passage he says, "I will": "For you have said in your heart: 'I will ascend into heaven, I will exalt my throne above the stars of God; I will also sit on the mount of the congregation on the farthest sides of the north; I will ascend above the heights of the clouds, I will be like the Most High'" (vv. 13, 14).

When the Enemy purposed this in his heart, a terrible thing happened to God's domain. Now two wills existed. Up until this time there had only been God's will, and everything moved in harmony and peace. God cannot allow any being to oppose His will and continue without punishment. The very essence of sin is to choose our will rather than God's.

When the Enemy came to Adam and Eve, he questioned the very will of God as it had been revealed by His spoken word. When man fell, there were three wills present in the universe. As Adam and Eve populated the earth, it became filled with hundreds, then thousands, then millions, and today billions of wills. This is why we are characterized as "sheep [that] have gone astray; we have turned, every one, to his own way" (Isaiah 53:6).

We are born as totally depraved human beings, naturally choosing our way rather than God's way. As the old McGuffey reader said, "In Adam's fall, we sinned all." The nature we are born with is a nature we have inherited from our ancient grandparent, Adam. It is a nature that consistently chooses what we desire rather than what God desires. It all began when one of God's angels said, "I will."

Satan has fallen, and the primeval sin of pride that brought him down still causes devastation on the earth. Mankind's desire for power, control, possessions, glory, and unrestrained conduct still causes all of our problems and conflicts.

Thank God Jesus has overthrown Satan. We must put away our pride and bow at Jesus' feet as our Lord and Savior. According to Scripture, one day Satan will be cast down at our feet (Ezekiel 28:17). One day he shall be gone forever: "Yet you shall be brought down to Sheol, to the lowest depths of the Pit" (Isaiah 14:15).

8

BATTLEGROUND PLANET EARTH

Now the serpent was more cunning than any beast of the field which the Lord God had made. And he said to the woman, "Has God indeed said, 'You shall not eat of every tree of the garden'?"

And the woman said to the serpent, "We may eat the fruit of the trees of the garden; but of the fruit of the tree which is in the midst of the garden, God has said, 'You shall not eat it, nor shall you touch it, lest you die.'"

Then the serpent said to the woman, "You will not surely die. For God knows that in the day you eat of it your

eyes will be opened, and you will be like God, knowing good and evil."

So when the woman saw that the tree was good for
food, that it was pleasant to the eyes, and a tree
desirable to make one wise, she took of its fruit and
ate. She also gave to her husband with her, and he
ate. Then the eyes of both of them were opened, and
they knew that they were naked; and they sewed fig
leaves together and made themselves coverings.

And they heard the sound of the Lord God walking
in the garden in the cool of the day, and Adam and
his wife hid themselves from the presence of the
Lord God among the trees of the garden.

Then the Lord God called to Adam and said to him,
"Where are you?"

So he said, "I heard Your voice in the garden, and I
was afraid because I was naked; and I hid myself."

And He said, "Who told you that you were naked?
Have you eaten from the tree of which I commanded
you that you should not eat?"

Then the man said, "The woman whom You gave to
be with me, she gave me of the tree, and I ate."

And the Lord God said to the woman, "What is this
you have done?"

The woman said, "The serpent deceived me, and I ate."

So the Lord God said to the serpent: "Because you have done this, you are cursed more than all cattle, and more than every beast of the field; on your belly you shall go, and you shall eat dust all the days of your life. And I will put enmity between you and the woman, and between your seed and her Seed; He shall bruise your head, and you shall bruise His heel" (Genesis 3:1-15).

Some believe that Lucifer, before his fall, was the principal being whom God had set over our created order. At his fall the primeval creation was ruined and enshrouded in darkness. Lucifer the light-bearer became Satan the adversary, or the Enemy. The shining cherub became the stalking dragon. Satan thought he was the source of his beauty, wisdom, and music. He was described as a jewel. This recognizes the fact that his glory could be seen only in pure light. In his pride he refused to see that his glory was a reflected glory. A diamond in total darkness is no more than a sharp pebble.

Thus, Satan received the verdict of heaven and was cast out in devastating judgment. He lost his position and authority. The creation now lies under devastating judgment and darkness. The following verses confirm this ruin: Job 9:3-10; 38:4-13; Psalm 18:7-15.

The scars of Earth tell of catastrophe. Two ancient ones are written across the face of this planet: the ancient ruin and the Flood. Look at the earth. It has been shaken. Continents have been torn apart. An age of ice and glacier has come. Deep canyons, shaky faults in the earth, unstable volcanoes, and earthquakes testify to the original ruin. The pre-incarnate Christ was the divine Creator. John 1:3 states: "All things were made through Him." Colossians 1:16, 17 states: "For by Him all things were created . . . and in Him all things consist [hold together]."

Satan's fall led to the devastation of the ancient creation. It was an attack on Christ before He became incarnate. The earth then lay for an unknown period of time as a wreck and a ruin. But God instituted His plan for the ruined creation. He would retake it through a creature to be known as man.

Thus, the stage is reset in Genesis 1 and 2. God, from existing matter, remade the earth and placed in it a paradise called Eden. Out of the chaos, God assembled order. In the six days of Creation we find terms such as "God made . . . divided . . . formed . . . set," and so forth. God used the material of the ruined creation. The word *create* is only used in reference to the "breath" of God. He created moving life out of existing materials, but made it live by His breath. Even man was formed of the "dust of the earth" and given life by God's creative Spirit.

So God made man in His own image. This means that man was given a spirit. This spirit had the three qualities of God: a mind to think, a heart to love, and a will to choose. He was placed in an environment which would test all three capacities. He could use his mind to name the animals and govern the earth. He could use his heart to love Eve and God. He could use his will to choose right or wrong.

In the midst of the garden stood the Tree of Life and the tree that led to death. Man was permitted to eat of all the trees, including the Tree of Life. The only restriction given to him was to avoid the tree that led to death—the Tree of Knowledge of Good and Evil.

At this point Satan embodied himself in a serpent. The Hebrew word for *seraph* means "fiery serpent" in Scripture. This image speaks of beauty and brilliance. (Only three times in Scripture does Satan take a body: in the serpent, in Judas Iscariot, and in the Antichrist.) Notice that Satan was already present on the earth! He launched his infernal attack on the crown of God's creation, man.

The Commencement of the War

The stage is set and Satan launches his attack on mankind. Notice two important things about Satan's attack in these verses of Genesis 3: his motive and his method of attack.

First, the motive of the Enemy can be seen. Why did Satan attack man? Because he viewed the creation of man as a mistake. He was, and is, jealous of the future glory that God has promised man. Psalm 8:5 says, "You have made [man] a little lower than the angels, and You have crowned him with glory and honor." Satan and his hosts of spirit beings desired the earth and its glory. They hated man and his position. Hebrews 2:7 states that God has "set [man] over the works of [His] hands." Satan's motive is to thwart God's plan on the earth.

Second, the method of the Enemy's attack is given. Satan attacked the first human beings. He sought to get to God through mankind. Satan always has a method. Ephesians 6:11 warns us of the "wiles of the devil." The word *wiles* is translated from the Greek word *methodeias,* or "methods."

Satan is deceptive but predictable. He used deception and temptations. Notice the steps of his seduction:

1. Doubt—"Has God indeed said. . . ?" (Genesis 3:1).
2. Denial—"You will not surely die" (v. 4).
3. Deception—"God knows . . . you will be like God" (v. 5).
4. Desire—"a tree desirable . . ." (v. 6).
   - Lust of the flesh—"tree was good for food"
   - Lust of the eyes—"pleasant to the eyes"
   - Pride of life—"to make one wise"

5. Death—"You shall surely die" (2:17).

This is the way Satan always operates. His methods of attack remain the same. He continues to have great success with them.

The Casualties of the War

Satan launched his attack through the woman. The Bible tells husbands to give honor to their wives "as to the weaker vessel" (1 Peter 3:7). This does not mean weaker in mind or body or endurance or worth; it means more susceptible. Satan approached Eve while she was away from her husband. She was completely deceived and thought that she was doing what was best for her husband. First Timothy 2:14 says that "Adam was not deceived." He knew exactly what he was doing. He chose by his own free will to disobey.

Through this act mankind became lost (Romans 5:12, 17, 19; 1 Corinthians 15:21, 22). At one point there had been only two wills: God's and Satan's. Now there are billions of wills. Every person has a will to choose for God or against God. Man is, by fact of nature and by choice of will, a sinner. Man is utterly lost.

The Continuation of the War

God announces continuous enmity between man and Satan. He is our adversary. It would seem as though Satan had won. He had deceived woman. He had succeeded in getting man to doubt the veracity of God's Word. He had succeeded in bringing doubt as to the goodness of God. But Satan failed at one decisive point—he could not govern the will of man. Isaiah 53:6 states it well: "We have turned, every one, to his own way." Man now asserts his fallen will. Satan cannot take the chaos of humanity and weld it together for long for his evil purpose.

This explains the terrible tragedies and difficulties of our world. This fallen world is under the curse of sin. Satan is a rebel against God, and so is every lost person. A war is going on. It is the nature of war to leave tragedy in its wake. Human history is a vast parade of both man and Satan trying to do something without God. God permits the horror of tragedy to convince an unbelieving world that it is utterly helpless without Him.

Jesus refused to pray for this present world. In John 17:9 He said, "I do not pray for the world but for those whom You have given Me."

The Climax Of The War

God announced ultimate triumph right from the beginning. There will be a wounded man and a crushed serpent, He said. Satan's defeat is to come through a Man.

The decisive battle took place on Calvary's cross. Satan vented his anger on the Son of God. Christ died for our sins to destroy Satan's demand for our souls. Satan held the power of death. But Hebrews 2:14 teaches the glorious truth that Christ suffered "that through death He might destroy him who had the power of death, that is, the devil."

Colossians 2:13-15 states that when we are saved we rest in the victory of Christ. He spoiled principalities and power. He robbed them of their powers. Satan has already been defeated.

It is our task, then, to enforce the victory of the Cross until Jesus comes for us. We don't belong to Satan. He has no authority over us. We are God's property. We simply affirm the fact now that all the kingdoms of this world are already overthrown. They are defeated and don't know it.

Ultimately all of Satan's invisible forces will be forever confined to the lake of fire. Until that day it is the purpose of God to display His glory in His new people, the church. Paul declared, "To make plain to everyone the administration of this mystery, which for ages past was kept hidden in God, who created all things. His intent was that now, through the church, the manifold wisdom of God should be made known to the rulers and authorities in the heavenly realms, according to his eternal purpose which he accomplished in Christ Jesus our Lord" (Ephesians 3:9-11, *NIV*).

God was not surprised by the fall of man. His plan is on schedule. Everyone who surrenders to Him and lays down the weapons of rebellion becomes a part of His new kingdom. We become soldiers as well as saints and servants until that day.

9

THE BELIEVER'S BATTLE POSITION

Finally, my brethren, be strong in the Lord and in the power of His might (Ephesians 6:10).

Operation Desert Shield in the 1991 Persian Gulf conflict was a classic example of battle strategy. No battle was launched until everything and everyone was in the proper position. Then air attacks began. The allied planes took the battle to the skies as the air attacks began. Then the ground troops moved in to recapture lost territory and set the captives free.

Spiritual warfare uses this same time-tested strategy. Believers must know their Enemy, know their own resources, and get into battle position. The proper battle position is described in Ephesians 6:10: "Be strong in the Lord." Salvation is Christ in you. Your exalted position is "you in Christ!"

Understand The Believer's Exalted Position

Paul's favorite description of a Christian is "in Christ." The Book of Ephesians uses this expression repeatedly to enumerate the privileges of being a Christian. Christians are to be "faithful in Christ Jesus" (1:1). The possibility of faithful living is ours because of our position in Christ. Also, "every spiritual blessing" is ours "in Christ" (v. 3). Our confirmation in the divine family is secured because "He made us accepted in the Beloved" (v. 6). In fact, if you read through Ephesians 1, you will discover that all that one needs for this life and the life to come is discovered by understanding what it means to be "in Christ." The focus is often on Christ being in the believer; yet, in Ephesians the believer is viewed as being "in Christ."

It is important to note that "in Christ" the believer has been exalted and enthroned above all principalities and powers. God has "raised us up together, and made us sit together in the heavenly places in Christ Jesus" (2:6). The "heavenly places" are where Christ is presently enthroned. God "raised Him from the dead and seated Him at His right hand in the heavenly places, far above all principality and power and might and dominion, and every name that is named, not only in this age but also in that which is to come. And He put all things under His feet" (1:20-22).

When we understand clearly our position in Christ, then we know that everything under His feet is also under the believer's feet. As ambassadors of heaven, believers have the authority of the throne of Jesus Christ! Our battle with Satan and his demons takes place in the heavenly places: "For we do not wrestle against flesh and blood, but against principalities, against powers, against the rulers of the darkness of this age, against spiritual hosts of wickedness in the heavenly places" (6:12).

You and I have no authority inherent within ourselves over demons. Yet, these wicked spiritual forces are fully aware of the authority that is ours in Jesus Christ. An American ambassador, though living away from his own country, still has citizenship here. When he speaks, it is with the authority of Washington, D.C., and all of the might of the United States. Likewise, we are citizens of heaven; here on earth we speak with all the authority of heaven.

Understand the Believer's Eternal Purpose

God's eternal purpose for every believer is Christlikeness. Our purpose is not to fight for a victory; our Lord has already won the decisive battle at Calvary. We fight *from His victory.* We are here to enforce the victory of the Lord. "Be strong in the Lord and in the power of His might" (v. 10).

The verb "be strong" is present passive imperative. It is a continuous command. Since it is passive, this indicates that the subject is strengthened by an outside power. It would be better translated, "Go on being strengthened." It is not the believer flexing his spiritual muscles; it is the believer receiving and appropriating God's strength.

God permits Satan to war against believers. Though this is a mystery, several reasons can be clearly noted:

First, warfare with Satan sharpens the believer's skill in using Scripture.

Second, these earthly battles are freeing us for exalted rule in the next world: "For I consider that the sufferings of this present time are not worthy to be compared with the glory which shall be revealed in us" (Romans 8:18).

Third, spiritual warfare teaches us the tragedy of the human conditions caused by the fall of mankind. Satan's hatred of the human race and his relentless efforts to control human destiny are clearly exposed in spiritual warfare.

Fourth, man learns his utter helplessness before evil without Christ. C.S. Lewis has said, "All that education and culture has done for man is to make him a more sophisticated and clever devil."

Fifth, spiritual warfare keeps the believer from becoming too comfortable in this world. Regular struggles with the Enemy remind us that we are living in hostile territory.

Finally, warfare teaches the believer that the servant is not above his master! Our Lord was a soldier. Even to the shedding of His blood, He battled and won (see chapter 6).

Now it is the believer's duty to enforce the victory Jesus has won. Our Lord was no stranger to warfare. He faced Satan at the beginning of His ministry when He was tempted, and at the end of His earthly ministry in the garden and on the cross. It is the purpose of God for every believer to know how to follow His example and do battle.

Understand the Believer's Power

"Be strong in the Lord and in the power of His might" (Ephesians 6:10).

A Christian who understands his position can begin to appropriate the power of Jesus. What is the "power of His might"? A similar phrase is found in Ephesians 1:19, 20. "The working of His mighty power" is the same power that raised the dead body of Jesus to life. It is the same power that exalted Him above all to the highest position in heaven and in earth. It is the same power Paul had in mind when he wrote, "I can do all things through Christ who strengthens me" (Philippians 4:13).

A person who accepts Christ as Lord is initiated into His victory. In this fierce and terrible war, we are in the winning position. How do we appropriate and apply His strength? The way is through prayer, the Word, and faith.

We appropriate unlimited power when we are willing to live for the Lord. The Spirit-filled life supplies the strength we need.

Satan has two major goals:

First, he desires to keep as many people as possible from salvation through Christ. Second Corinthians 4:4 gives us Satan's terrible strategy: he blinds unbelievers "that they might not see the light of the gospel of the glory of Christ, who is the image of God" (*NASB*).

Satan believes that his only hope of reprieve is to damn so many human beings that God will reverse His plan of redemption and thus prove to be unrighteous.

Second, Satan desires to neutralize believers by defeating and discouraging them. Wake up to the truth! If you do not take your battle position in Christ, the Enemy will destroy you. Right now, take your position in Christ.

Pray with me this prayer:

Heavenly Father, I bow in praise and ownership before You. I praise You that the blood of Jesus is my covering. I praise You for the Holy Spirit who indwells and fills my life.

I surrender myself anew to You as living sacrifice. I repudiate conformity to this world and praise You for the transforming work of Christ.

I renounce Satan and all his workers, and declare that they have no right to interfere with me in this prayer. I am praying to the true and living God and refuse any involvement of the Enemy in this prayer.

I ask You, Lord, to rebuke Satan, and I now take my exalted position in Christ. I recognize that the armor of God is none other than Christ! My sword is the Word of God and praise.

I praise You, Jesus, that in this position, on Your throne, the Enemy is under my feet. I reject, repudiate, and renounce all that Satan has brought against me. I bring the blood of Jesus against him and command him to leave in the name of Jesus Christ. I call all principalities and powers to take notice that I know who I am in Christ. I will live in Christ and over Satan in Jesus' sure victory. In His strong name, amen.

10

THE DEMONIC DYNASTY

For we do not wrestle against flesh and blood, but
against principalities, against powers, against the
rulers of the darkness of this age, against spiritual
hosts of wickedness in the heavenly places
(Ephesians 6:12).

J oy Adamson, the naturalist and author, was the
wife of a game warden in East Africa. One day in
1956 her husband brought home three lion cubs that
had been left to their own defenses when their mother
was killed.

Joy Adamson nurtured the three cubs until they were grown and released them into the wild. She then told the story of Elsa, one of the lionesses, in a book titled *Born Free*. Other books followed: *Living Free* and *Forever Free*. The books were best-sellers, and each was made into a popular motion picture.

Apparently Joy Adamson forgot she was dealing with wild beasts capable of destruction. At the age of 69, while at a camp 30 miles from a telephone, she was attacked and killed by a lion. The animals she had befriended became her enemy.

Do not make the mistake of thinking you can tame Satan, the tormentor. You cannot have peaceful coexistence with the Enemy. Sooner or later, he will destroy the careless and foolish.

A real war is going on against a real Enemy! Once we assume our position in Christ, then the next step is to know the Enemy so that we can be properly equipped. Let us examine the dangerous infernal army at Satan's disposal. Revelation 12:9 reaches back before time: "So the great dragon was cast out, that serpent of old, called the Devil and Satan, who deceives the whole world; he was cast out to the earth, and his angels were cast out with him." These fallen angels are variously referred to in Scripture as "demons," "principalities," "powers," "rulers of darkness," "wicked spirits," "unclean spirits," and other names. According to Revelation 12:4 a third of the innumerable hosts of angels fell: "His [Satan's] tail drew a third of the stars of heaven." "Stars" are symbolic of the angels.

The Infernal Army Arrayed Against Us

Jesus Christ confronted demons as an integral part of His ministry. When He launched His ministry, He quoted Isaiah 61:1, 2, which is cited in Luke 4:18: "The Spirit of the Lord is upon Me, because He has anointed Me to preach the gospel to the poor; He has sent Me to heal the brokenhearted, to proclaim liberty to the captives . . . to set at liberty those who are oppressed." Obviously Jesus saw His ministry as rescuing humanity from the bondage and oppression of the Enemy.

At least nine times in the New Testament, Jesus confronted demons. In the next two chapters more details will be given about demonic operation, but first we will look briefly into an incident in the life of Jesus and learn something about demons. The beloved physician, Luke, recorded his version of the demoniac of the Gadarenes:

> Then they sailed to the country of the Gadarenes, which is opposite Galilee. And when He stepped out on the land, there met Him a certain man from the city who had demons for a long time. And he wore no clothes, nor did he live in a house but in the tombs. When he saw Jesus, he cried out, fell down before

Him, and with a loud voice said, "What have I to do with You, Jesus, Son of the Most High God? I beg You, do not torment me!" For He had commanded the unclean spirit to come out of the man. For it had often seized him, and he was kept under guard, bound with chains and shackles; and he broke the bonds and was driven by the demon into the wilderness.

Jesus asked him, saying, "What is your name?"

And he said, "Legion," because many demons had entered him. So they begged Him that He would not command them to go out into the abyss.

Now a herd of many swine was feeding there on the mountain. So they begged Him that He would permit them to enter them. And He permitted them. Then the demons went out of the man and entered the swine, and the herd ran violently down the steep place into the lake and drowned.

When those who fed them saw what had happened, they fled and told it in the city and in the country. Then they went out to see what had happened, and came to Jesus, and found the man from whom the demons had departed, sitting at the feet of Jesus, clothed and in his right mind. And they were afraid. They also who had seen it told them by what means he who had been demon-possessed was healed. Then the whole multitude of the surrounding region of the Gadarenes asked Him to depart from them, for they were seized with great fear. And He got into the boat and returned.

Now the man from whom the demons had departed begged Him that he might be with Him. But Jesus sent him away, saying, "Return to your own house, and tell what great things God has done for you." And he went his way and proclaimed throughout the whole city what great things Jesus had done for him (Luke 8:26-39).

Notice the demons in these verses. Demons have personality and speed, seem to express the emotion of fear, promote uncleanness, torment, and create mental disorders. Yet, the glorious truth is that demons must obey the commands of Jesus Christ.

Can a Person Be Demon-Possessed?

The Greek word describing the condition of a person affected by a demon is *daimonizomai*. This word is translated "demon-possessed" in the *New King James Version*. According to Arndt and Gingrich, it is present tense with an active voice and a passive ending. A person in this condition can be described as influenced by "a demon-controlled passivity." In other words, the person is controlled by a demon to a point of passivity. C. Fred Dickason rightly points out that the term *possession*, in relation to demons, never appears in the New Testament. A demon can possess an unbeliever. However, a believer can be oppressed by the Enemy.

Demons can use people's voices, confuse, give imaginations, create insanity, appear as multiple personalities, and cause passivity of speech, hearing, and physical movement.

In Jesus' confrontation with demons, we observe such feats as unusual physical strength, fits of rage, multiple and disintegrating personalities, resistance to Jesus, clairvoyance (they knew who Jesus was), and occult transference (the demons entered swine). Some of these phenomena will be discussed in greater detail later.

Kurt Koch, an eminent German pastor, and psychiatrist Alfred Lechler researched demonization in Germany. They noted the demonized individuals' resistance to the Bible, their trancelike state, their resistance to prayer, and their negative reactions to Jesus' name.

Do Demons Affect Christians?

One of Satan's great strategies is to convince believers that they are immune to demonic influence. A Spirit-filled believer walking in obedience to Christ is absolutely protected from the Enemy. A disobedient Christian may still have his or her spirit protected from the Enemy. However, the mind and body of an unfaithful Christian is subject to attack.

A Christian can "give place to the devil" (Ephesians 4:27). When a Christian lives with unconfessed, habitual sin, the Enemy moves in to that place in the believer's life. The Enemy erects a thought pattern around that sin or attitude. That "house" of thoughts is described as a "stronghold" in 2 Corinthians 10:4, 5. Demons can live in that stronghold in the life of the believer. (See chapter 21 for a complete discussion on strongholds.)

These demons do not possess the Christian any more than a cockroach can possess a house. They can harass, oppress, depress, and suppress the believer. Demons cannot damn the Christian, but they can distract the Christian. In the next two chapters we shall expose their operation so that as a believer you can be alert.

The Believer's Need for Spiritual Armor

In Ephesians 6:11 the believer is commanded to "put on" (enduo) the whole armor of God. In verse 13 he is told to "take up" (analambano) the whole armor of God.

Enduo means "to clothe oneself once and for all." Analambano means "to be commanded to dress for the battle immediately and finally." Only then has the believer "done all, to stand," and only then is he prepared "to withstand" (v. 13).

Having looked at Satan's infernal arsenal, let us now look at our eternal arsenal. We are not to disarm, but rather to be armed for the battle. God has given us an armory of both offensive and defensive weapons. In later chapters we will discuss in detail each piece of spiritual armor. However, it is important for us to see the armor as a unit. Each piece of the armor is an attribute of Jesus. The believer must appropriate all of the power and character of Jesus. Though Jesus is always in us, we may not be aware that we are in Him. It is possible to live beneath our privilege and be bombarded by the Enemy.

Six pieces of armor were drawn from that worn by the Roman soldier. The entire panoply presents the character of the spiritual warrior: honesty is pictured by the belt, purity by the breastplate, stability by the shoes, faith by the shield, assurance by the helmet, and power by the sword of the Spirit (vv. 14-17). (See chapters 13-18 for a full discussion on the armor.)

Obviously a believer can be unaware of the armor, or fail to appropriate it. Demons can indeed operate in believers who live wayward lives. The duty of every Christian is to be dressed up in the full armor of God.

Six Things the Enemy Cannot Do

Let me encourage every Christian to live a life of holiness and spiritual awareness before God. When one is right with God, the Enemy is totally ineffective against him or her. Following are some of the actions the Enemy cannot take:

1. *The Enemy cannot penetrate the blood of Jesus.* Revelation 12:11 declares, "They overcame him

[Satan] by the blood of the Lamb." The blood has been applied to your spirit. When the Holy Spirit controls your life, then all of your life is under the blood. When the flesh controls your life, it is open season on your unprotected mind and body!

2. *The Enemy cannot harm the believer in full armor.* When we stand up in the armor of Jesus, demons flee before us. When we are only full of ourselves, then the Enemy can come.

3. *The Enemy cannot read your mind, though he can sow seeds of thought.* The Enemy often operates on the basis of what he hears you say. When you confess negative ideas, like "I am getting sick," the Enemy hears that and dispatches demons to assist you in getting sick. One might see a task for God and say, "I cannot do that." Immediately, a demon will come and reinforce what has been said.

4. *Demons cannot and will not leave unless you speak to them.* Demons must be exposed and expelled.

5. *Demons cannot thwart the ultimate will of God.* It may seem at times that Satan's forces have the upper hand. The skirmishes they may seem to win do not affect the sovereign will of God.

6. *A demon cannot and will not confess Jesus to be Lord this side of eternity.*

The Methods of Satan

As you study the Scriptures you will learn that demons are highly intelligent and well organized. Ephesians 6:11 speaks of "the wiles of the devil." The word *wiles* is translated from the Greek word *methodeia*, from which our English word *method* is drawn. It means "schemes and plans." Satan has a plan to do what he wants done. His two major tasks are to damn people and to make believers ineffective.

Demons Use Deception

Revelation 12:9 declares that Satan has deceived the whole world. The word *deceive* pictures a person who believes a lie to be the truth. A deceived person is one who is utterly convinced that right is wrong and wrong is right. Satan is a deceiver. He practices his deception in many realms. Basically, deception is practiced in the area of the Word of God. If Satan can convince a person that God is a liar, then he can get that person to violate God's principle of living. The other area of deception is on the person and work of Christ.

Demons use perversion to distort the plan of God. Satan is a perverter of all the physical appetites that God has given us. The appetite for food may be perverted into gluttony. Alcohol given by God as a medicine has been perverted into the worst social problem in America (see Proverbs 20:1; 23:1-3, 20, 21, 29-35). Sex is God's gift to a man and woman in the bond of marriage. Now this gift has been perverted into every wickedness imaginable. The Scripture forbids pre-marital sex and homosexual acts; Satan says they are acceptable. The world calls it "sexual preference."

Satan perverts the plan of God. Satan produces imitators who misuse the plan of God and lead people astray. When Moses stood before Pharaoh and his rod became a serpent, the magicians did the same thing (Exodus 7:11-22). There has been and will be many wolves in sheep's clothing until the return of Christ. Satan will ultimately produce the Antichrist who will be an imitation of Jesus.

Therefore it is necessary to test the spirit that speaks out of a man. Test it by the Word of God: "Beloved, do not believe every spirit, but test the spirits, whether they are of God; because many false prophets have gone out into the world" (1 John 4:1).

Satan's greatest device against Christians is that which he used against Job: namely, accusation. Satan will accuse us of sin which God has forgiven. He is a slanderer and a liar. He accused Job of serving God for material blessings. Job was vindicated and God was victorious. Satan used the weather, death, family, disease, and false friends. Through it all, Job neither cursed God nor charged God wrongly.

Satan will tell you that God is to blame for your trouble. He will tell you sin is to blame. He will accuse you and try to defeat and destroy your faith. Our defense is confession of sin according to 1 John 1:9. We are not condemned; we are forgiven.

Perhaps one of the greatest tools Satan operates in the world is rebellion against authority. Human government was permitted in order to thwart Satan's purpose of lawlessness. When rebellion and anarchy overthrow a government, it always brings a more repressive regime. The breakdown of authority in the nation, home, and church will bring a harsher government or total destruction. The bombing of New York City's World Trade Center in 1994 and the tragic bombing of the federal building in Oklahoma City in 1995 are clear examples of demonically inspired rebellion.

The Bible warns us of the sin of rebellion. Saul's rebellion is described as witchcraft and his stubbornness as iniquity and idolatry (1 Samuel 15:23). Satan destroyed Saul by rebellion. It is a dangerous thing not to live under authority. Churches would do well to take heed to the Word concerning living under God-given authority.

Other methods Satan uses include temptations of the flesh, occult involvement, religious charlatans, fear, and intimidation.

The victory belongs to the believer who will take the resources provided by God. Only the unarmed will know defeat! When Eliot Ness first began fighting the Capone mob in Chicago, the FBI was not allowed to carry weapons. Only after a number of agents were killed did the government finally agree to allow them to be armed.

Our King has permitted us to bear arms! Let us clothe ourselves with God's armor and live in victory!

11

UNMASKING DEMONIC OPERATIONS

When an unclean spirit goes out of a man, he goes through dry places, seeking rest; and finding none, he says, "I will return to my house from which I came." And when he comes, he finds it swept and put in order. Then he goes and takes with him seven other spirits more wicked than himself, and they enter and dwell there; and the last state of that man is worse than the first (Luke 11:24-26)

Having exposed the demonic dynasty in the last chapter, let us look more deeply into demonic

personality and operation. Remember, Satan's kingdom is in direct conflict with the kingdom of God.
Though defeated, Satan still holds sway in this world.
In Matthew 4:8, 9, Satan offered the world and its
power and glory to Jesus. First John 5:19 says, "The
whole world lies under the sway of the wicked one."
Satan has innumerable demonic forces at his disposal.

In this strange passage in Luke 11:24-26, Jesus
spoke of the operation of these demonic entities. This
is the clearest picture of demonic thinking in all of
Scripture. Look carefully at these verses and you will
note the following disturbing facts about demonic
operation. (I am indebted to booklets of the late
Earnest Rockstad for help with this section.)

1. *Demons can exist both inside and outside of
human beings.* It is clear that demons can pass
through the atmosphere of this planet.

2. *Demons travel at will.* Verse 24 says that they
go "through dry places, seeking rest." They seem to
prefer traveling over land rather than water. In Mark
5, Jesus dispatched the demons in the swine into the
sea of Galilee.

3. *Demons desire to be embodied in order to rest.*
They go "through dry places, seeking rest." It seems
that demons are weary until they find a human host.
They prefer to inhabit a human being.

4. *Demons can communicate with us by using the vocal apparatus of their hosts.* On many occasions demons spoke from the bodies of their hosts. Luke 11:24 makes it clear that demons can speak. In the incident in Mark 5 they spoke through the human host.

5. *Demons have individual personalities and identities.* Notice that in Luke 11:24 the demon says, "I will." Demons are not impersonal forces, but like the angels they have names and personalities.

6. *Demons consider the body they live in to be their home!* The demon in this passage says of his former human host, "I will return to my house from which I came." Demons are possessive and seek to take ownership of the human lives they invade. Think of it, a demon bragging to his cohosts that your body is his house! This is why Paul warns us in Ephesians 4:27 about giving "place to the devil." Give the Enemy a foothold and he will put up a mailbox and declare your body his address.

Some years back there was a movie called *Pacific Heights*. In this movie a young couple purchase a large home and remodel it. In order to meet the mortgage, they rent out part of it to a man. He refuses to pay rent, he harasses the couple, he sues them, and he makes their lives a living hell. The house was possessed by a mad man who took over their lives!

109

That story graphically illustrates the strategy of demons. A demon will come in quietly to live in that little area of your life that you refuse to surrender to Jesus. From that stronghold he will try to rule and ruin your life.

7. *Demons can plant thoughts and influence mental health.* Luke 11:25 makes a reference to the human mind: "And when he comes, he finds it swept and put in order."

The demon returns to the person who has been set free. He finds the mind clean and in order. Yet this person has no spiritual fullness. The Holy Spirit is either not present in that person's life or is not filling his mind and controlling his body.

This host has gone back to the same sin. Perhaps anger was the stronghold from which he had been delivered. Instead of growing in the Lord, filling the mind with Scripture and living in praise, this individual falls into the same pattern and the demon can see the emptiness in the person. Demons attack the mind that is devoid of God.

8. *Demons can remember, think, and plan.* Notice in all these verses the strategies employed by these evil beings. They are not stupid and must not be regarded lightly.

9. *Demons can communicate with each other.* In verse 26 this demon communicates with seven others.

When one gives place to a demonic power, that power will often bring compatible demons. The Bible speaks of the "spirit of fear" (2 Timothy 1:7). In 1 John 4:18 we read that "perfect love casts out fear, because fear involves torment." Jesus spoke of tormentors in Matthew 18:34, 35, in regard to those who will not forgive. So a demon of fear can bring demons of torment. Unforgiveness can invite tormentors into a person's life. Demons, like roaches, tend to increase in number if not evicted. Only the power of God can evict the demons.

10. *Levels of evil exist within the demonic hierarchy.* Luke 11:26 says that the demon "takes with him seven other spirits more wicked than himself." Demonic spirits exist in various levels of wickedness. Here, one demon enlists seven more to occupy his hosts. If a person tolerates a little evil, more evil will soon come.

11. *Demons are a problem to Christians today.* Ephesians 6:12 says we are in a hand-to-hand wrestling match "against principalities, against powers, against the rulers of the darkness of this age, against spiritual hosts of wickedness." Although these spirits cannot possess a Christian's spirit, they can afflict the body and oppress the mind. We must be ever vigilant to enforce the victory of the Cross on these evil forces.

12. *Demons are involved in deceiving believers by teaching false doctrine.* "Now the Spirit expressly says that in latter times some will depart from the faith, giving heed to deceiving spirits and doctrines of demons" (1 Timothy 4:1). In these last days demons are seducing and deceiving many through false teaching. Just because a person waves a Bible and acts spiritual does not mean that his ministry is God-anointed. Religious deception is the worst of all demonic control.

In concluding this chapter, let it be clear that ignoring the truth about the demonic forces is frivolous and perilous. By not facing the truth about our Enemy, we leave ourselves and the church ill-prepared for the battle that rages. How many spiritual casualties will it take before the church wakes up to the reality of spiritual warfare?

12

14 SYMPTOMS OF DEMONIC OPERATION

All mental illness is not the result of demonic attack. Further, good psychological care from Christian professionals is vital and in order. Also, professionally administered medication may be necessary when chemical imbalances occur. As these symptoms are listed, realize that some of them could also be caused by other than demonic oppression. When normal medicine and therapy do not result in help or a cure, then it is possible that these symptoms could point to demonic operation. The first six symptoms are extreme and are drawn from the account of the demoniac of Gadara in Mark 5.

This man had been chained in a cemetery because of his erratic and violent behavior. When you look at Mark 5:1-15 you can see clear symptoms of demonic activity.

Symptom 1: Incapacity for Normal Living (Mark 5:1-5)

The actions of Legion made him unsuitable for normal social interaction with friends and family. An unusual desire for solitude, accompanied by a deep loneliness, will often set in. The person will often become very passive with no desire to change.

Symptom 2: Extreme Behavior (Mark 5:4)

Violent behavior will often be evident in the victim's life. An explosive temper and extreme uncontrollable anger will often be observed in the victim's life.

Symptom 3: Personality Changes (Mark 5:9, 12)

Multiple personalities exist in some of the most serious cases of demonic control. This man had a "legion" of spirits within his life. All cases of multiple personality may not be demonic, but in most cases demon activity is involved. Changes in personality, extreme or mild, may be evidence of the activity of a demon.

Symptom 4: Restlessness and Insomnia (Mark 5:5)

In verse 5 we see this man crying in the tombs "night and day." He could not sleep. Insomnia can be a sign of a physical problem or a sign of a spiritual problem. God has gifted His children with sleep (Psalm 127:2). When we cannot sleep, often the reason may be that we are sick, God wants to talk to us, or the devil is tormenting us. You have the right in Jesus to rest!

Psalm 3 is a picture of warfare. Here David was hounded by his enemies. In verses 3, 4, he cried to the Lord, "You . . . are a shield for me." In verses 5, 6, he cried, "I lay down and slept; I awoke, for the Lord sustained me. I will not be afraid of ten thousands of people who have set themselves against me all around." He also said in Psalm 4:8, "I will both lie down in peace, and sleep; for You alone, O Lord, make me dwell in safety." Sleep is God's gift to all who trust in Him.

Symptom 5: A Terrible Inner Anguish (Mark 5:5)

Obviously the man in this context was deeply tormented in mind and heart. Various levels of anguish are evident in those who are afflicted by demons.

115

Grief and anguish are normal emotions for us all. Yet, persistent unresolved anguish that will not leave after normal therapies of counseling, encouragement, and prayer could well be demonic.

Symptom 6: Self-inflicted Injury and Suicide (Mark 5:5)

In Mark 5:5 the demonic man was cutting himself. Mark 9:14-29 tells the story of the man whose son was both deaf and mute because of a demon. Verse 18 says, "Wherever it [the evil spirit] seizes him, it throws him down." Verse 22 continues, "Often he [the demon] has thrown him [the boy] both into the fire and into the water to destroy him." Jesus cast out the demon. "The spirit cried out, convulsed him greatly, and came out of him. And he became as one dead. . . . But Jesus took him by the hand and lifted him up, and he arose" (vv. 26, 27).

Demons can cause people to injure themselves. They even incite suicide.

Symptom 7: Unexplained Illness With No Obvious Medical Cause

Sometimes these illnesses are psychological, and good counseling can result in a cure. Sometimes the battle is with the mind and emotions and not with demons.

116

On the other hand, we find in Luke 13:11-16 the story of a woman afflicted by a "spirit of infirmity" (v. 11) whom Jesus called "a daughter of Abraham, whom Satan has bound" (v. 16). Obviously, she was a child of God, faithful to her synagogue, with a desire to know more about the Lord. "Jesus . . . said to her, 'Woman, you are loosed from your infirmity.' And He laid hands on her, and immediately she was made straight, and glorified God" (vv. 12, 13). There are physical illnesses caused by a class of demons known as "spirits of infirmity."

Symptom 8: Addictive Behavior

Addictions to alcohol, drugs, sex, food, gambling, and other things open the door to demonic influence and control. I am not saying demons cause all of these problems; certainly people are responsible for their own wrong choices. But anything that causes one to be out of control opens that person to infernal control.

Symptom 9: Abnormal Sexual Behavior

When Jezebel's son inquired about peace in 2 Kings 9, Jehu responded, "What peace, as long as the harlotries of your mother Jezebel and her witchcraft are so many?" (v. 22).

In Ezekiel 16:20-51 the spirit of harlotry is mentioned several times. This spirit infected the nation of Israel with the sins of Sodom (vv. 49, 50). They even sacrificed their own children (vv. 20, 21).

Homosexuality, adultery, fornication, and even infanticide were all inspired by the spirit of harlotry. Hosea 4:12 says, "The spirit of harlotry has caused them to stray, and they have played the harlot against their God." Look at 5:4: "They do not direct their deeds toward turning to their God, for the spirit of harlotry is in their midst, and they do not know the Lord."

A nation and a people given over to sexual sins and abominations is governed by this spirit of harlotry. We must battle this principality that dominates our nation. Look at Nahum 3:4: "Because of the multitude of harlotries of the seductive harlot, the mistress of sorceries, who sells nations through her harlotries, and families through her sorceries."

Nations and families are sold into spiritual bondage by the witchcraft of the spirit of harlotry. When we play around with sexual sin, we open ourselves to this demonic spirit.

Symptom 10: Defeat, Failure, and Depression in the Christian Life

In 2 Corinthians 2:14 Paul said, "Now thanks be to God who always leads us in triumph in Christ."

Many have never noticed that this verse follows verses 10 and 11, which exhort us to forgive others "lest Satan should take advantage of us; for we are not ignorant of his devices." It is Satan's purpose to get an advantage over us in order to rob us of the victorious life that is ours in Christ. The psalmist cried out, "By this I know that You are well pleased with me, because my enemy does not triumph over me" (Psalm 41:11).

This symptom is often manifested by an inability to praise and worship. Psalm 92:1-4 is a testimony to the power of praise. It culminates in verse 4, where David said, "For You, Lord, have made me glad through Your work; I will triumph in the works of Your hands." Again, "Save us, O Lord our God . . . to give thanks . . . [and] to triumph in Your praise" (106:47).

Symptom 11: Occult Involvement and Behavior

Deuteronomy 18:9-12 catalogs the works of the occult and witchcraft, mentioning such acts as child sacrifice, witchcraft, fortune-telling, soothsayers, interpreters of omens, sorcerers, those who conjure spells, mediums, spiritists, and those who call up the dead.

119

Verse 15 says that to the contrary, the people were to hear the word of God from the prophet of God and order their lives accordingly. Occult involvement is clearly a symptom of demonic controls.

Symptom 12: Speech Difficulties

In Matthew 9:32, 33, Jesus rebuked a demon and the mute man was able to speak. Speech difficulties may be physical, emotional, mental, and in some cases demonic. Extreme language and cursing may be prompted by the Enemy.

Symptom 13: Doctrinal Error

First Timothy 4:1 warns us that in the last days deceiving spirits will teach the doctrines of demons. Today, religious cults and charlatans abound. The reason these deceivers draw many people is the power of the demonic that teaches them.

Symptom 14: Religious Legalism

Galatians 3:1 says to the believer who is in danger of going back under the law: "Who has bewitched you that you should not obey the truth?" The church at Galatia had forsaken a faith ministry that resulted in the miraculous (v. 5) for a law ministry of rules and regulations. Paul classified this error as witchcraft.

Some deeply religious people are under the bondage of tradition, man-made rules, and outward appearances. Demons thrive in this kind of environment, especially demons of control. It is a lot easier to keep a ritual or list of rules than it is to walk by faith. Wherever there is any substitute for faith in the finished work of Christ, it is a doctrine of demons.

PART THREE

THE WARRIOR EQUIPPED

13

THE INTEGRITY OF THE WARRIOR

Stand therefore, having girded your waist with truth. . . . (Ephesians 6:14).

The old hymn "Stand Up for Jesus" has a line in it that goes like this: "Put on the gospel armor, each piece put on with prayer." This thought reflects what Paul is saying to the church. Having declared the believers' position for battle in verse 10 and their posture for battle in verses 11-13, Paul moves to their panoply for battle.

Both verses 11 and 13 command the believer to "put on" or "take up" the whole armor of God. This once-and-for-all command includes the entire outfit. The Greek word *panoplia* comes from *pan*, meaning "all," and *hopla*, meaning "weaponry." The *panoplia* ("whole armor") includes all of the soldier's equipment. One scholar translates it, "Put on the splendid armor."

When Paul wrote the Book of Ephesians, he wrote from personal knowledge about Roman soldiers. He was chained to one under guard when he wrote: "I, Paul, the prisoner of Christ Jesus . . ." (3:1); "I, therefore, the prisoner of the Lord, beseech you . . ." (4:1). He described himself as "an ambassador in chains" (6:20). Paul saw in the Roman soldier a wonderful illustration of spiritual truth.

Understand that the armor is symbolic. The armor is no less than Christ himself. Every believer knows Christ as Savior. The problem comes when we do not appropriate all our Lord brings with Him. You see, it is not Christ available, but Christ appropriated, that makes the difference. Romans 13:14 says, "Put on the Lord Jesus Christ, and make no provision for the flesh, to fulfill its lusts." The term "put on" is translated from the same Greek word, *enduo*, found in Ephesians 6:11. Paul wrote to Timothy, "Be strong in the grace that is in Christ Jesus" (2 Timothy 2:1).

In the battles of life Christ is the answer, but His resources must be appropriated.

In the greater context there are three pieces of armor that should always be in place without question: the belt, the breastplate, and the boots (Ephesians 6:14, 15). The other pieces are to be taken up decisively and finally. The emphasis here is that it is possible to forget these pieces of armor, such as the shield, helmet, and the sword. We are to take these up regularly into the battle. But in this chapter we will focus on the belt of truth.

The Belt of Truth Displays an Illustration of Integrity

The belt served three primary purposes for the Roman soldier.

1. It held all of his weapons and equipment together.

2. It was used to tie his robes so that he would not trip going into battle.

3. It was ornamental, displaying medals or awards for heroism in battle.

Here it is a spiritual weapon, but the functions are the same. It is called a belt of truth, therefore it pictures the Lord Jesus Christ who said, "I am . . . the truth." It also pictures the written Word of God that keeps one from tripping over the obstacles in the world. Finally, it pictures the honesty and integrity that ought to characterize the life of all who know Jesus Christ.

The Belt of Truth Exhibits the Inspiration for Integrity

As we have already observed, the Lord Jesus Christ is the armor for the believer. Isaiah 11:5 said of Him, "Righteousness shall be the belt of His loins, and faithfulness the belt of His waist."

When Jesus faced Satan, He declared the truth of the Word of God (Matthew 4). He looked at the Pharisees who opposed Him and said, "Which of you convicts Me of sin?" (John 8:46). Pilate looked at Jesus and asked, "What is truth?" And then he declared, "I find no fault in Him" (18:38). Even the thief on the cross cried, "This Man has done nothing wrong" (Luke 23:41).

Our Lord Jesus Christ spoke the truth and lived the truth. He remains the truth today. Revelation 1:12, 13 pictures Jesus in His glorified state: He is bound, or girded, by a golden belt. All of our Lord's glory is bound together by His truth.

The belt represents the Lord Jesus Christ and His Word holding everything together in one's life. His truth, His character, and His integrity are to characterize our lives.

A music student walked into his teacher's studio and asked, "What good news do you have today?" The teacher picked up a hammer and hit the tuning fork. He said, "That note is A; it will be A tomorrow; it was A 5,000 years ago. It will be A 5,000 years from now."

Life can hold together only if it is bound together by unchanging truth. Jesus Christ and His Word are the tuning forks that give our lives harmony in a discordant world.

The Belt of Truth Teaches Us the Importance of Integrity

This belt of truth is displayed in the honesty and integrity of the believer. Our lives ought to be lived in such a way that people see the truth. Just as the Roman soldier used the belt to bind his robe to keep from tripping, so the truth of Jesus' Word keeps us from tripping before a watching world.

Also the believers' medals of victory worn on the belt of integrity are their reputations. Ephesians 4:14-16 warns the believer of false doctrine and deceptive teachers. Verse 15 challenges us to speak "the truth in love" so that we "may grow up in all things."

How do we learn to tell the truth, to live honestly? According to verses 17-25, Jesus teaches us to live honestly. There are three basic areas where we tend to be dishonest in our lives:

Divided living. We are warned in Scripture of trying to live a divided, hypocritical life.

Dishonest finances. Matthew 6:21 warns, "For where your treasure is, there your heart will be also." Our hearts must be in the right place. The heart is the affections. The location of our affections will be illustrated by what we do with our money.

Double-minded thinking. James 1:8 says, "He is a double-minded man, unstable in all his ways." This causes unstable living. Matthew 6:24 warns us that "no one can serve two masters." This speaks of having divided allegiance. This person serves God one day and the world the next.

Jesus alone can teach us to live the truth. We must deal with our hearts, our minds, and our wills.

You and I can be blameless. Philippians 2:12-16 declares that the secret of living out our salvation is God at work in the believer. If we yield to Him so that He can truly work in us, we can be "blameless and harmless, children of God without fault in the midst of a crooked and perverse generation, among whom you shine as lights in the world, holding fast the word of life" (vv. 15, 16).

Sir Philip Sydney was engaged in a fierce battle. He saw one of his fellow soldiers remove his leg armor, so Sydney removed his leg armor too. Later, Sydney received a fatal wound in the leg where the armor had been removed.

Let us remember that our Enemy can move in to destroy us in the area of honesty and character.

Do you know the truth in a Person? Jesus is the truth. You can call on the great philosophers, but Socrates, Plato, and Kant will not answer. You can call on great leaders of the past and they will not answer. Jesus Christ will answer you today. He proved His truthfulness by rising from the dead. You must admit the truth about yourself and receive the truth of Jesus today. When you do, integrity will characterize your life.

14

THE HEART OF
THE WARRIOR

Stand therefore . . . having put on the breastplate of righteousness (Ephesians 6:14).

The second piece of armor needed by soldier-saints is the breastplate of righteousness. The Greek word for *breastplate* is *thorax*. This piece of armor was made of metal and leather, fastened around the soldier's body from the neck to the thighs. It protected one's vital organs, including the heart and lungs.

In the armor of the believer, it is called the "breastplate of righteousness." The word *righteousness* literally means to be made right or to be justified. The internal organs were considered by first-century people to be the center of will and emotions. Spiritually, a blow to the mind and emotions is very dangerous. Satan desires to "mess up" your mind. He is an accuser and a slanderer.

What is the righteousness that protects our minds and hearts? First, we will consider what it is not.

Realize There Is an Impotent Righteousness

"We are all like an unclean thing, and all our righteousnesses are like filthy rags" (Isaiah 64:6). Romans 3:10ff cites several Old Testament passages, declaring, "There is none righteous, no, not one." From these passages we know that this righteousness is not self-righteousness.

This righteousness is not a natural human attribute. This righteousness is not religious activity, charitable activity, or human goodness. Our very best behavior is tainted by sin.

Vance Havner has called human righteousness "the good that is not good enough." Jesus said, "Unless your righteousness exceeds the righteousness of the scribes and Pharisees, you will by no means enter the kingdom of heaven" (Matthew 5:20).

Pharisees lived good lives outwardly. Paul was a Pharisee before his conversion. His testimony in Philippians 3:4-9 was that as a Pharisee he was religious, had zeal, and was blameless.

What does all of this mean? Simply this: you can never be righteous (right with God) on your own merits!

How then can a person be righteous?

Receive an Imputed Righteousness

Jesus said, "But seek first the kingdom of God and His righteousness, and all these things shall be added to you" (Matthew 6:33). His reign and His righteousness are necessary in our lives. How can we obtain "the righteousness of God"?

Romans 3:19-26 tells us clearly that Jesus Christ is the righteousness of God. "Being justified freely by His grace through the redemption that is in Christ Jesus, whom God set forth as a propitiation by His blood, through faith, to demonstrate His righteousness" (vv. 24, 25).

The only dilemma God ever faced was to be righteous and make sinners righteous at the same time. This dilemma was solved when Christ became the blood sacrifice for the sins of humanity. He died to pay the penalty and bear the curse of the law against all of us.

Romans 3:21, 22 declares that the righteousness of God is revealed and received.

Second Corinthians 5:21 tells us how this is possible. "For He made Him who knew no sin to be sin for us, that we might become the righteousness of God in Him." Scripture declares that we are righteous because He has imputed His righteousness to us. "And if anyone sins, we have an Advocate with the Father, Jesus Christ the righteous" (1 John 2:1). Scripture also says that we are righteous "just as He is righteous" (3:7).

Romans 5:17-19 declares that this righteousness of God is a gift of God's grace. Further, this gift enables us to reign in life. The righteousness of Jesus marks us as royalty!

All of these scriptures declare that righteousness is a gift of God and a work of God. Righteousness is the Son of God in our lives. You receive this righteousness by faith. God said it, you believe it, and that settles it!

Respond as Instruments of Righteousness

If righteousness is a gift of God, why are we told to put on righteousness? Righteousness must not only be declared, it must also be demonstrated. It must not only be accepted, it must also be appropriated.

"Even the righteousness of God, through faith in Jesus Christ, to all and on all who believe" (Romans 3:22).

Notice that this righteousness is not only "to all," but it is to be "on all."

By faith we must act on the fact of our current position. Satan will accuse and slander the believer over sin which has already been forgiven (see 2 Corinthians 2:10, 11). He will call us everything but who we are in Jesus. Furthermore, Satan tempts us to use our bodies for unrighteousness (Romans 6:13). Satan cannot impugn the righteousness of Jesus!

Rest in an Impregnable Righteousness

Few believers understand who they are in Jesus. Receiving His righteousness gives us a new identity. After we have received or acknowledged His righteousness, then it becomes our defense. It defends our vital organs. Amy Carmichael said that "nothing anyone can do to us can injure us unless we allow it to cause a wrong reaction in our own spirits."

A breastplate was designed to deflect the blow of the enemy. The righteousness of Christ protects the believer in the same way. When you have accepted Jesus and you know that He has accepted you, this deflects the arrows of rejection by others. When you know that God sees you as 100 percent righteous, this deflects the put-downs, the guilt, and accusations of the Enemy.

This righteousness protects from inferiority. Identity with Christ is the key to a healthy self-image.

The world says, "You are nothing," but God says, "You are royalty" (see Romans 5:17).

The Enemy says, "You have no future," but God is preparing for you to reign with Him in glory.

The devil will tell you that you are unimportant and what you do is insignificant. Someone said, "All born-again believers, as members of the future bride of Christ, are fully as significant, important, and of great consequence in God's ongoing undertakings, adventures, and creative endeavor, as any intelligence in the universe."

We cannot control others. Satan will come against us with all kinds of attacks. The only way he can get through is if we react wrongly. When we respond in the wrong way—whether it be in anger, pouting, self-pity, or self-rejection—we have failed to appropriate the breastplate of righteousness.

Only what touches your spirit can really injure you. If you allow what happens to you, or what is said to you, to affect what God has said about you, then you are not using the breastplate.

What motivated the Prodigal Son to get out of the hogpen? He realized who he was: he was a son! When he came home his father said, "This my son was dead and is alive again" (see Luke 15:32).

The breastplate of righteousness protects from immorality. When we know that we are righteous in Jesus and will share in His reign, we do not want to live beneath our position. Why should an heir of God want to live like an animal? Why should a saint want to be a reprobate? Why would a king want to live like a slave?

There was a day when a person would live right to protect the family name. When we realize that we have Jesus and that He is our righteousness, then this motivation enables us to live out what we are in Jesus. You are not a sinner saved by grace; you *were* a sinner. Now you are a saint and a family member. Why would you live less than you are?

By an act of will we can yield our bodies to be controlled by His righteousness (Romans 6:13). The righteousness of Jesus controls our behavior.

This righteousness protects from insecurity. "The kingdom of God is not meat and drink; but righteousness, and peace, and joy in the Holy Ghost" (Romans 14:17, KJV). "Seek first the kingdom of God and His righteousness, and all these things shall be added to you" (Matthew 6:33).

When Jesus is king in our lives, then we are the beneficiaries of His righteousness. All of the rest of life will fall into place. The things that happen in our lives may be God's way of saying, "Recognize My reign and receive My righteousness."

What do you need to do? Pray the following prayer:

Lord, I have no righteousness of my own. I give You my sin for Your righteousness.

Lord, I receive Your righteousness as my standing before the Father. I gladly confess that I am now, and forever will be, who You say I am. I confess to being Your child, a saint, an heir of God, a part of Your bride and body.

Lord, I yield my body as an instrument of righteousness. I recognize that all I was in Adam is now dead and that all I am in Jesus makes me Your own.

Lord, I accept the Bible as Your very breath of life. I acknowledge 2 Timothy 3:16, which tells us that all Scripture is God-breathed and is profitable for instruction in righteousness.

Lord, I thank You that Your death has made me righteous before the Father.

15

THE WALK OF
THE WARRIOR

And having shod your feet with the preparation of the
gospel of peace (Ephesians 6:15).

Jesus Christ himself is the armor of God. "Put on
the Lord Jesus Christ" (Romans 13:14). Putting on
the armor is simply realizing who Jesus is, recogniz-
ing who you are in Him, and appropriating all He has
for your life.

The piece of armor we will consider in this chapter
is the warrior's shoes. Great generals have said that

in warfare an army moves on two vital things: its food and its feet. This was especially true of the Roman army, which had to march great distances over rugged terrain. The Roman battle dress for the foot was a thick leather sole with hobnails to serve as cleats. It was tied to the feet and leg with leather laces.

These boots served three purposes:

1. *To provide firm footing.* The nails dug into the ground to keep the soldiers from slipping.

2. *To furnish protection.* In those days the enemy would drive pegs into the ground and sharpen the tips. A barefoot soldier would receive a painful puncture wound in the foot. Infection would set in and disable the soldier.

3. *To give mobility.* These shoes made it possible for the army to move quickly to the place of battle.

Our spiritual shoes serve essentially the same purpose. They help us see clearly what solid foundation is under us and what keeps us moving.

The Identity of the Shoes

The believer's spiritual warfare shoes are described as "the gospel of peace." We stand on the sure foundation of the gospel. *Gospel* means "good news." What is the "good news"? In 1 Corinthians 15:1-4, Paul described the gospel as the death, burial, and resurrection of Christ. Our firm footing is the unchanging message of Jesus Christ. There are still some unchanging and unalterable truths.

Many people are slipping and sliding in their faith. Many substitutes are offered for the gospel. Paul confronted this problem in Galatians 1:6-10. This false gospel had the following marks: it was different, it was perverted, it was accursed, and it pleased men.

We live with the same problems:

- We have the *social gospel*, which teaches that if we improve a person's living conditions, educational level, and outlook, we give the person salvation. This does nothing to change the heart.

- We have the *works gospel*. It teaches that if we do our best for our neighbor and try to help others, God will save us.

- We have the *New Age gospel*, which teaches a one-world government run by the highest and best of human philosophy. This doctrine prepares the world for Antichrist and damnation, not for salvation.

- We have the *health and wealth gospel*. This is the "God-wants-you-rich" philosophy. We have seen thousands duped by this false approach.

- We have the *gospel according to humanism*. Humanists believe in the goodness of man. This "Pollyanna" approach to sinful humanity is fatally flawed.

Galatians 5:1 says, "Stand fast therefore in the liberty by which Christ has made us free." We have but one gospel and one way to be saved: "Nor is there salvation

143

in any other, for there is no other name under heaven given among men by which we must be saved" (Acts 4:12; see also vv. 10, 11). This is where we must stand.

The Stability of the Shoes

This is a day of spiritual tumbleweeds, blown about by circumstance and false doctrine. Shoes give us stability to keep us from stumbling in the battle. It is possible, even in the battleground of this world, to live a stable life. Our text speaks of the gospel of peace.

The word *peace* is translated from the Greek word *eirene*. The Hebrew word is *shalom*. Peace is a state of well-being, a sense of contentment. I can have peace with God while I am at war with the devil himself. "Therefore, having been justified by faith, we have peace with God through our Lord Jesus Christ, through whom also we have access by faith into this grace in which we stand, and rejoice in hope of the glory of God" (Romans 5:1, 2).

When you know that you stand before God at peace with Him because of the blood of Jesus, then Satan cannot worry you to death. W.D. Cornell must have been experiencing God's peace when he wrote the words to "Wonderful Peace."

> Peace, peace, wonderful peace
>
> Coming down from the Father above.
>
> Sweep over my spirit forever, I pray,
>
> In fathomless billows of love.

If you allow the devil to trouble your mind and cause you anxiety, then all of your life becomes unstable. James 1:8 warns us, "A double-minded man [is] unstable in all his ways." Don't allow the Enemy to take your shoes off. Remember, in Christ you have what the world longs for—peace (Romans 5:1, 2) and true freedom (Galatians 5:1).

The Mobility of the Shoes

The word *preparation* is translated from a Greek word which means "readiness." The idea is of one being ready to move into battle at a moment's notice.

Already in Ephesians we have learned that the Christian life is a walk:

- We are not to walk wrongly (2:2).

- We are to walk in His works (2:10).

- We are to walk worthily (4:1).

- We are to walk in love (5:1, 2).

- We are to walk in the light (5:8).

You cannot walk properly without your gospel shoes in place. Too many Christians are sluggish and slow-footed. Others who have walked in the world without their shoes on are wounded and crippled. Today the church is paralyzed and muscle-bound.

Before World War II, General Charles de Gaulle wrote a book warning France that a new kind of warfare was coming. The French had built the Maginot Line on their border. This defensive line consisted of powerful weapons in place facing Germany. De Gaulle warned the nation that new weapons, such as fighter planes and tanks, would make their defenses obsolete. No one listened and France became a captive nation.

Churches that draw their own lines of defense will stand still. We must be ready to advance with the gospel. Our opportunity for service is today. Now we must use our resources for spreading the gospel of Jesus Christ. We must be ready to move to the front where the battle for souls rages. Let us not flinch in this battle.

We must stand on the secure footing of the truth about Jesus. We must stand with stability of heart, even in the midst of our conflicts. We must be ready to move and stand in the heat of the battles.

Achilles, a hero of Greek mythology, was wounded in his heel. This was the only part of his body exposed, yet the wound killed him. Our feet must not be left unshod if we are to survive and triumph.

16

THE FAITH OF
THE WARRIOR

Above all, taking the shield of faith with which you
will be able to quench all the fiery darts of the wicked
one (Ephesians 6:16).

In the ancient wars, archers would dip their arrows
in pitch, set the tips of the arrows on fire, and launch
them toward the opponent. The unwary soldier
struck by one of these flaming missiles would receive
an agonizing wound. Their clothing would often be
ignited and they would be severely burned.

To combat these fiery arrows, the Romans invented a large door-shaped shield. The shields would measure four feet by two feet. Leather would be stretched around the frame; and prior to a battle, the shields were soaked in water. This served to repel the fiery arrows of the enemy.

Paul used this weapon to illustrate faith. He changed the verb in the Greek language from *having* to *taking* to describe the believer's use of the last three weapons (vv. 16, 17). One can "take" the shield, the helmet, and the sword. This means that one may choose to appropriate faith or not to appropriate faith.

What is faith? New Testament faith is believing to the point of commitment. Faith is trusting and acting on what God has said. Faith is as valid as the object on which it rests. Here faith is said to be a shield. A shield like this was used by the Roman soldier to defend against the enemy as well as to advance against the enemy. If I am to put my faith in a shield, I need to know more about that shield.

The Shield Taken

In order to take the shield, you must understand what—or rather who—the shield is in Scripture. We discover in Genesis 14, and 15 the identity of our shield. In these chapters, Abraham wins a great victory. The king of Sodom offers him a reward which he wisely refuses. Rather, Abraham pays tithes to Melchizedek shortly after Abraham refused the reward of the world. God speaks to him and says, "Do not be afraid, Abram. I am your shield, your exceedingly great reward" (15:1).

Abraham put his life in God's hands. God was the shield he needed in order to live in a hostile world.

David also took the shield of faith. He said, "But You, O Lord, are a shield for me" (Psalm 3:3). In Psalm 84:11 we read, "For the Lord God is a sun and shield; the Lord will give grace and glory; no good thing will He withhold from those who walk uprightly."

We take the shield of faith when we trust the Lord. Habakkuk 2:4 says, "The just shall live by his faith." Habakkuk wrote this at a time when the wicked prospered, the enemy threatened, and the people of God needed revival. He asked God hard questions. God's answer was "Live by faith." This verse is quoted in Romans 1:17, Galatians 3:11, and Hebrews 10:38. Faith not only gives us life, but it is the way we live our lives.

We are saved by faith in God's Word about His Son. We also live by faith: "The life which I now live in the flesh I live by faith in the Son of God, who loved me and gave Himself for me" (Galatians 2:20). The songwriter expresses his thoughts this way:

O worship the King, all glorious above,
And gratefully sing His wonderful love;
Our Shield and Defender, the Ancient of Days,
Pavilioned in splendor, and girded with praise.

The Shield Tested

The test of faith reminds us of the "wicked one," whom we meet daily on the battlefield of our lives. This should not surprise us or alarm us. Our Lord was tested by the Enemy in the wilderness temptation. When the apostle Paul wrote of this shield of faith, he was in prison.

The shield of faith does not protect us from life. Paul faced difficult circumstances, bodily weaknesses, exhausting labors, agonizing disappointments—yet he had a shield. You may go through trials of faith, but God won't let anything touch you without His permission. The shield is not meant to make you comfortable in this world. The shield is Christ, and we face everything by His grace.

The devil will hurl his fiery darts. They come sometimes as temptation. They come as distractions. They come as accusations. They come as imaginations. They come as depression. Sometimes they come as persecution! All of these flaming arrows of hellish hate can be answered by Jesus. This Shield can take care of all that Satan can hurl at you.

How does faith answer the attacks of the Enemy? With the Word of God, always! Faith rests on the character of God, the Word of God, and the promise of God.

When Satan accuses you, let the Word of God answer Him. Let the cross of Christ answer the Enemy. Refuse the flaming missiles of the Enemy.

Someone may ask, "What if I can't remember a scripture?" Just cry out for God. When a child is in trouble and does not know what to do, the child cries, "Daddy." Dear friend, when you don't know how to answer, just cry out for God!

The Shield Triumphant

All that Satan can hurl at a believer, God can take care of. "This is the victory that has overcome the world—our faith" (1 John 5:4). Faith is always victorious.

Often the Roman army would place their best soldiers on the front line. On occasion that line would stretch a mile. The army would advance behind that phalanx of brave soldiers who would go forward behind the shield.

The church advances behind the mighty shield of faith. Without faith we are defenseless and useless to God. We cannot please Him without faith. Faith alone is the key to victory. Faith is how we live. Faith is "frontline" Christianity. Faith protects us from Satan. Faith appropriates the promises of God. Faith is always victorious.

17

THE MIND OF THE WARRIOR

Take the helmet of salvation . . . (Ephesians 6:17).

Every believer is a saint and a soldier—a worshipper and a warrior—in the faith and in the fight! As warriors we fight from a position of strength and victory. We wage war in the right posture, for we are told to stand! We are supplied with a panoply of armor that is adequate to carry us through the battlefields of this life.

We face an intelligent, aggressive Enemy who targets the crucial areas of our life for attack. The Greek word for *devil* (*diabolos*) means "a traducer, false accuser, slanderer." He is the "one who hurls through." He is an accuser.

God has provided armor with which to defend our faith and defeat our foes. This armor is comprised of the attributes of our Lord Jesus Christ:

- When you receive the *belt of truth*, it is Jesus who says, "I am . . . the truth" (John 14:6).

- When you receive the *breastplate of righteousness*, it is Jesus who is the righteousness of God (1 Corinthians 1:30).

- When you put on the *shoes of peace*, it is Jesus who says, "My peace I give to you" (John 14:27).

- When you lift the *shield of faith*, it is Jesus alone who can answer every fiery accusation of hell.

Next is the *helmet of salvation*. The Roman helmet, made of metal, covered the head and the cheekbones. It protected against the death blow of the enemy. The "helmet of salvation" likewise protects the believer from the death blow of Satan. Let us look at Satan's attack on the mind.

The Attack on the Mind

We live in a corrupt world in which people are governed by a "reprobate mind" (Romans 1:28, KJV). Believers are warned not to walk "in the vanity of their mind" (Ephesians 4:17, KJV).

George Bernard Shaw said, "The science to which I pinned my faith is bankrupt. In science's name I helped destroy the faith of millions of worshippers. Now they look at me and witness the tragedy of an atheist who has lost his faith."

Our world talks about "safe sex" rather than about moral living. Our nation knows a lot about rights and not much about responsibility. Even the church often runs its ministry according to the world. Romans 8:6 says, "To be carnally minded is death." "Carnally minded" means to think according to the flesh.

In Luke 12:29 Jesus warned us about the confused mind: "Neither be ye of doubtful mind" (KJV). The word *doubtful* is translated from the Greek word *meteorizo*, from which our English word *meteor* comes. It means to be "up in the air, suspended, unsettled." There are many who have allowed their lives to be without answer.

Philippians 4:6 says, "Be anxious for nothing."

Much discouragement and depression is caused by needless worry. Our minds must not be filled with deception. Second Corinthians 2:11 warns us about a careless mind: "We are not ignorant of his [Satan's] devices." How foolish to live in ignorance of Satan's deceptions. God wants us to think straight.

The Assurance of the Mind

The helmet is called the "helmet of salvation." Salvation is the deliverance of the believers from their lost and condemned position, to life in God's kingdom. Salvation has three perspectives:

1. *Salvation is a past event.* In the counsels of eternity, at the Cross in history, and in one's personal conversion, salvation is an event that begins in the past.

2. *Salvation is a present experience.* Salvation continues in the life of the Christian. "He who has begun a good work in you will complete it until the day of Jesus Christ" (Philippians 1:6). Salvation goes on happening in the life of the Christian.

3. *Salvation is a promised expectation.* Salvation looks ahead to the believer's future hope. Romans 13:11 speaks of that future perspective: "Now our salvation is nearer than when we first believed."

I am convinced that the helmet of salvation is our assurance of God's protection until the day He comes back. In 1 Thessalonians 5:4-9, the helmet is clearly defined as the "hope of salvation." We can keep our heads straight and our minds from being messed up by remembering that the Lord is in control and that He is coming.

Psychiatrists tell us that for good mental health, a person needs someone to love, something worthwhile to do, and something to hope for. This is true on a practical level. Knowing that Friday is coming gets some of us through the week. The knowledge that present pain will end and health will come gets people through illness and surgery.

The hope of heaven and a better life helps to carry us through this life. Titus 2:13 says, "Looking for the blessed hope and glorious appearing of our great God and Savior Jesus Christ." Hebrews 6:18, 19 says, "That . . . we might have strong consolation, who have fled for refuge to lay hold of the hope set before us. This hope we have as an anchor of the soul." The Forerunner, our Lord, has gone before us to glory and anchored our souls to His throne. There is nothing the world can do that our anchor of hope cannot get us through.

The Answer of the Mind

How do we control, then, our thoughts and minds?

First, one must repent in the mind. Repentance comes from the Greek word *metanoia,* which means "a change of mind."

Second, one must receive with the mind. "Let this mind be in you which was also in Christ Jesus" (Philippians 2:5). "We have the mind of Christ" (1 Corinthians 2:16). "Since Christ suffered for us in the flesh, arm yourselves also with the same mind" (1 Peter 4:1).

Third, one must renew the mind. "Present your bodies a living sacrifice, holy, acceptable to God, which is your reasonable service. And do not be conformed to this world, but be transformed by the renewing of your mind, that you may prove what is that good and acceptable and perfect will of God" (Romans 12:1, 2). These verses teach us that surrendering our bodies to Him and refusing to be conformed to the world brings the renewal of the mind. This is a daily need.

Steps to a Renewed Mind

How does one renew the mind? Philippians 4:4-13 sets forth the steps to handling troubled thoughts and a messed-up mind.

The first step is to rejoice in the Lord. "Rejoice in the Lord always. Again I will say, rejoice! Let your gentleness be known to all men. The Lord is at hand" (vv. 4, 5). Praise is a great antidote to trouble. Rejoicing acknowledges the nearness of the Lord.

The second step is for the believer to request of God. "Be anxious for nothing, but in everything by prayer and supplication, with thanksgiving, let your requests be made known to God" (v. 6). Prayer is an antidote to mental agony. Talk to God about your needs.

Third, the believer can rest in Christ. "The peace of God, which surpasses all understanding, will guard your hearts and minds through Christ Jesus" (v. 7). Let God's peace stand guard over your mind.

Fourth, one can reflect on the good things of God. "Whatever things are true, whatever things are noble, whatever things are just, whatever things are pure, whatever things are lovely, whatever things are of good report, if there is any virtue and if there is anything praiseworthy—meditate on these things. The things which you learned and received and heard and saw in me, these do, and the God of peace will be with you" (vv. 8, 9). Think good thoughts. Use the Bible to counter the evil thoughts.

Finally, one can relax in the Lord. "But I rejoiced in the Lord greatly that now at last your care for me has flourished again; though you surely did care, but you lacked opportunity. Not that I speak in regard to need, for I have learned in whatever state I am, to be content: I know how to be abased, and I know how to abound. Everywhere and in all things I have learned both to be full and to be hungry, both to abound and to suffer need. I can do all things through Christ who strengthens me" (vv. 10-13).

God has promised to supply all our needs. Faith thanks God and receives from His hand all that we need.

Are you wearing the helmet of salvation? Are you living in hope? Is your mind clear? Are you thinking straight? Jesus Christ will give you a new mind. Do you need to repent? Do you need to receive? Do you need to renew your mind? Jesus Christ stands ready to help you today.

18

THE WEAPONS OF THE WARRIOR

And take . . . the sword of the Spirit, which is the word of God; praying always with all prayer and supplication in the Spirit, being watchful to this end with all perseverance and supplication for all the saints (Ephesians 6:17, 18).

This section on warfare calls on every Christian to stand against Satan. Now, Satan comes at us directly—through the world system in which we live and through our flesh. All of the weapons that we have studied thus far are defensive in nature. With these weapons we can fend off the attack of our Enemy:

- With our belt and breastplate we have integrity and identity in Christ. Satan cannot attack our character.

- With our shoes and shield we have balance and belief. Satan cannot penetrate our commitment.

- With our helmet we have assurance and anticipation of the good things of God. Satan cannot destroy our confidence.

James 4:7 tells us, "Resist the devil and he will flee from you." Defensive weapons can hold off Satan, but only offensive weapons can cause him to flee! God has supplied just such a weapon in the sword of the Spirit.

The word *sword* is used of the Roman two-edged sword, one used in hand-to-hand combat. This perfectly balanced weapon was handled skillfully by the Roman soldiers who practiced several hours daily to perfect its use. Let us learn about this weapon and its use.

The Sword and the Soldier

Take . . . the sword. The word *take* is an aorist imperative middle verb in the Greek text. It is a once-

and-for-all command for the soldier-saint to take what God has available. The offensive weapon God offers is His Word. The Word of God is to be used to attack our enemy, Satan.

This sword is not of human origin. It was forged by the divine decree. It was not tempered with earthly fire, but in the burning flames of the majestic Presence. The hammer of heavenly inspiration shaped the sword that fits in the hand of the believer.

Hebrews 4:12, 13, says that the Word of God is a living sword. It is penetrating and powerful. The sharp sword of the Word of God exposes evil. In this passage the sword is in the hand of our great High Priest, the Lord Jesus. Using the sword as a surgical tool, He can cut into our lives and discern the thoughts and intentions. With this sword He performed the surgery of salvation.

After using the sword on you, the saint, Jesus places the same sword in your hand. The secret of King Arthur's fighting ability was his sword, "Excalibur." This special sword endowed an ordinary warrior with extraordinary power! So it is with the believer. The sword of the Spirit gives the believer a weapon of unlimited power.

The Sword and the Spirit

Take . . . the sword of the Spirit. Notice carefully that the sword is connected to the Spirit of God. Having the sword of the Spirit is not simply having a Bible! The Holy Spirit inspired the Bible (2 Peter 1:21). Only the Holy Spirit can teach you the Bible: "The Counselor, the Holy Spirit, whom the Father will send in my name, will teach you all things" (John 14:26, *NIV*). John 16:13 says of the Spirit, "He will guide you into all truth."

Without the Holy Spirit the truths of the Bible cannot be understood. "The natural man does not receive the things of the Spirit of God, for they are foolishness to him; nor can he know them, because they are spiritually discerned" (1 Corinthians 2:14). The power of the Holy Spirit directs the use of the Word in the life of the believer.

In 2 Timothy 3, Paul wrote about the perilous times that are coming in the last days. He encouraged Timothy not to be defeated by persecution. What weapon did Paul place in the hand of Timothy?

- In verse 15, he encouraged Timothy to remember the "Holy Scriptures," which he had known from childhood.

- In verse 16, Paul spoke of the wonderful inspiration of the Scriptures: "All Scripture is given by inspiration of God, and is profitable for doctrine, for reproof, for correction, for instruction in righteousness."

In 4:2, he told the young preacher, "Preach the word!" Only the Word of God will get you through.

The Sword and the Struggle

Take . . . the sword of the Spirit, which is the word of God (Ephesians 6:17). How can we use the sword? In our text the phrase translated "word of God" is, in the Greek, the *rhema* of God." The normal word for "word" is *logos*, which means the whole of God's Word. The word *rhema* is the practical application of the Word. The Bible becomes a sword when the Spirit applies it to your life and through your life.

Jesus illustrated this truth in His temptation in Matthew 4. Every assault by Satan was answered with Scripture. Jesus did not argue with Satan; He answered him with the potent Word of God. How did Jesus apply the Word? Remember that Jesus had been praying and fasting for 40 days. According to Ephesians 6:18, the sword is effective through the means of prayer. When Israel battled the Amalekites, Moses prayed while the soldiers fought. Aaron and Hur went up to the top of the hill and held up Moses' arms until the victory came (see Exodus 17:8-12).

167

The Sword and Supplication

Prayer is not an additional weapon, but rather the essential life of the spiritual soldier. Prayer is not something to add to the Christian life, it is absolutely essential for victory. Armor does not help if a person has no courage and strength to battle.

Verse 18 gives a complete lesson on prayer.

The occasion of prayer. "Praying always with all prayer." Prayer is spiritual breathing that brings life to the soul. Believers are exhorted to "watch and pray" (Mark 14:38). Jesus said, "Men ought always to pray, and not to faint" (Luke 18:1, KJV). Praying with the sword of the Spirit includes every kind of praying: adoration, confession, thanksgiving, and intercession.

The omnipotence of prayer. Prayer must be more than words, more than a speech to an audience directed at God. Real prayer takes place only when it is Spirit-directed. The Bible is the sword of the Spirit, and prayer is the hand of the Spirit that wields the sword. Romans 8:26, 27 teaches us that the Holy Spirit prays for us and helps us to pray: "Likewise the Spirit also helps in our weaknesses. For we do not know what we should pray for as we ought, but the Spirit Himself makes intercession for us with groanings which cannot be uttered. Now He who searches the hearts knows what the mind of the Spirit is, because He makes intercession for the saints according to the will of God."

The Holy Spirit is "the Spirit of grace and supplication" (Zechariah 12:10).

The obligation of prayer. This prayer life must be consistent. It must be alert. It must include all believers. When is the last time you prayed for believers in other lands? How the church needs a worldwide concert of prayer!

You and I must take the Word of God and its promises to the prayer closet. Whatever your weakness may be, go to the Scriptures and begin to memorize and apply them by prayer.

Another way to use the sword is to praise. Psalm 149:6 says, "Let the high praises of God be in their mouth, and a two-edged sword in their hand." Every one of us needs to take the sword of the Spirit. The Word of God must be loved, learned, and lived out, in order for it to be a sword. No part of our lives should be lived without prayer and the Word.

In 2 Samuel 23:10, we are told about Eleazar, one of David's mighty men. He fought the Philistines until the sword stuck to his hand. That sword became an extension of his body. May the Word of God, the sword of the Spirit, be that and more to all who would be good soldiers of Jesus Christ.

19

FIVE UNFAILING RESOURCES OF THE WARRIOR

Therefore submit to God. Resist the devil and he will flee from you (James 4:7).

And they overcame him [Satan] by the blood of the Lamb and by the word of their testimony, and they did not love their lives to the death (Revelation 12:11).

In this chapter, we will summarize and organize the truths God has revealed to us. Five unfailing resources guarantee us spiritual victory.

The Authority of Our Position in Christ

When we were saved, Paul declares in Ephesians 2:6, we were raised up with Christ and seated with Him in the heavenlies. In Ephesians 1:20-22, we discover that principalities and powers are under our feet when we assume our rightful authority in Christ.

The believer is vested with this authority by virtue of his union with Christ. This authority is exercised by the power and authority of the indwelling Holy Spirit. We must stand against the Enemy with a firm, unfaltering faith. We must not be afraid to confidently command the Enemy to leave our presence and stop interfering with our lives.

The Word of God

In the New Testament two Greek words are translated "word" in reference to Scripture. One is the word *logos*, which means the Word in all of its meaning and understanding. *Rhema* is the other expression and it means the Word spoken and applied; it means the Word unleashed. Ephesians 6:17 calls the Word "the sword of the Spirit." "Word" in this verse is *rhema*, which means the Word spoken, applied, unleashed, and released. Satan and his demons will flee before the armed believer who speaks forth the Word of God. Our Lord Jesus, when tempted by

Satan in the wilderness, used only the Scripture to drive him away (Matthew 4:1-11).

Prayer and Fasting

In Ephesians 6:18, the believer who is attired in the full panoply of armor is instructed to be "praying always with all prayer and supplication in the Spirit." In extreme cases, prayer should be accompanied by fasting. In Mark 9:14-29 Jesus encountered a desperate father with a demonized son. While Jesus was on the Mount of Transfiguration, His disciples waiting for Him below failed in their efforts to bring deliverance to the boy.

The issue was one of faith: "If you can believe, all things are possible to him who believes" (v. 23). Jesus cast out the demon and then challenged His disciples, saying, "This kind can come out by nothing but prayer and fasting" (v. 29).

Fasting must be a discipline for Christians who engage in spiritual warfare. Isaiah 58:6-12 defines fasting as giving up one's own possessions in order to help the needy. This kind of fasting is one of God's chosen ways to defeat the Enemy. "Is this not the fast that I have chosen: to loose the bonds of wickedness, to undo heavy burdens, to let the oppressed go free, and that you break every yoke?" (v. 6). Prayer and fasting are effective against the Enemy.

Praise and Worship

In the Old Testament, praise was used as a weapon. Second Chronicles 20 records the story of Jehoshaphat and his battle against the Ammonites and Moabites. The following strategy was used for victory:

- Fervent prayer is offered by the leader to God (vv. 1-13).

- Earnest attention is given to the message from God, as proclaimed by a Spirit-filled man of God (vv. 13-17).

- Praise and worship goes out first against the enemy (vv. 18-22). Jehoshaphat instructed the choirs to sing "with voices loud and high" (v. 19). As they praised "the beauty of holiness" (v. 21), the invisible hosts of God moved into battle formation. "Now when they began to sing and to praise, the Lord set ambushes against the people of Ammon, Moab, and Mount Seir, who had come against Judah; and they were defeated" (v. 22).

Psalm 149:6 says, "Let the high praises of God be in their mouth, and a two-edged sword in their hand." Praise is a strong weapon against the Enemy.

174

The Presence and Virtue of the Lord Jesus Christ

Four vital truths about Jesus guarantee victory in your life.

First, you have the blood of Jesus for your sins. First John 1:7 says, "The blood of Jesus Christ . . . cleanses us from all sin." Satan and his demons can only penetrate where unconfessed sin gives them a place. The blood is a sure weapon. "And they overcame him [Satan] by the blood of the Lamb" (Revelation 12:11).

Second, you have the cross of Jesus to take care of your flesh. "Those who are Christ's have crucified the flesh with its passions and desires" (Galatians 5:24). This identification with Christ's cross takes you out of the sin-enjoying business. Galatians 2:20 says, "I am crucified with Christ: nevertheless I live; yet not I, but Christ liveth in me: and the life which I now live in the flesh I live by the faith of the Son of God, who loved me, and gave himself for me" (KJV). The indwelling Christ operates through the believer who lives by faith.

Third, we have the name of Jesus for defeating the Enemy. In Acts 16:18, Paul cast the demon out of a young girl, commanding the spirit "in the name of Jesus Christ to come out of her." In the Bible, "in the name of" represents the character and authority of a person. The name of Jesus Christ is not a magic word; it is the recognition of Jesus' awesome presence and power in every situation.

Philippians 2:10 says, "That at the name of Jesus every knee should bow, of those in heaven, and of those on earth, and of those under the earth." Obviously demons must bow to the name of Jesus Christ.

Fourth, faith in Jesus is our sure protection. Ephesians 6:16 speaks of "taking the shield of faith with which you will be able to quench all the fiery darts of the wicked one." Christians must believe God in the face of the Enemy's accusations, in the crises of circumstances, and in the storms of difficulty.

Faith keeps us believing in God when something is not so until it becomes so . . . because God said it is so!

PART FOUR

THE JOURNEY TO FREEDOM

20

COMING HOME FROM BONDAGE

When the Lord brought back the captivity of Zion, we were like those who dream. Then our mouth was filled with laughter, and our tongue with singing.

Then they said among the nations, "The Lord has done great things for them." The Lord has done great things for us, and we are glad. Bring back our captivity, O Lord, as the streams in the South.

Those who sow in tears shall reap in joy. He who continually goes forth weeping, bearing seed for sowing, shall doubtless come again with rejoicing, bringing his sheaves with him (Psalm 126:1-6).

In a seminar Dr. Neil Anderson said, "No more than 15 percent of the church community is enjoying the freedom and joy that's available to them in Christ!" What should the Christian life be like? The late Vance Havner, noted speaker and author, said, "The average Christian is so subnormal that when he sees normal Christians, he thinks they are abnormal."

When a believer discovers his identity in Christ, puts on the whole armor of God, and begins to live in his rightful heritage of freedom, what is it like? I believe it is like Israel's return from their ordeal and captivity in Babylon, which portrays the results of this freedom so beautifully.

Psalm 126 was written to celebrate the return from Babylon to Zion. In this psalm we observe the five legacies of liberty. These facets of freedom will be clearly seen in the life of the individual, or in the life of the church, that has been liberated.

Freedom in Christ Is Like a Dream Come True

When the Lord brought back the captivity of Zion, we were like those who dream (v. 1). The Christian life experienced to its fullest is also a dream come true. Most believers are living far beneath their privileges.

Jesus promised, "I have come that they may have life, and that they may have it more abundantly" (John 10:10). Are you living with an abundance of power, resources, and joy? The supernatural power of God is our heritage. The fruit of the Spirit is our promise.

Having led hundreds of people to freedom in Christ, I can say honestly that for many of them life becomes new, fresh, and exhilarating. One young lady was suffering from anorexia nervosa, a self-destructive starvation. Although she had seen some counselors, her problem was not physical but spiritual. After extended counseling she rejected the Enemy and his deception. The truth set her free. She is now active for Christ and especially enjoys singing in the choir.

People who have been set free from the Enemy's strongholds invariably experience an amazing awakening to the spiritual life. Suddenly, their eyes are open to all that they have in Christ.

In the early 50s, before cruises became the vogue, a poor man booked a passage from London to the United States in order to see his family. On board he stuck to himself and never entered the dining room. Toward the end of the journey, passengers asked him why he did not eat in the dining room. "Oh, I could afford only a ticket for the trip. But I brought along cheese and crackers to sustain me," he assured them.

"Why man, the food is included in the price of the ticket!" his fellow passenger said. It is possible to live the Christian life that way. We must realize that our commitment to Christ has brought us all that we need for this life and the life to come.

Christian Freedom Is a Source of Joy

Then our mouth was filled with laughter, and our tongue with singing (v. 2). Never have I seen more joyless people than in the average church or religious gathering. People seem restrained, and bound by tradition, denomination, or religious pride. Where is the exuberance, the wholehearted singing, the joyful shout, and the sounds of laughter?

No wonder so many believers and churches are insipid and weak. Nehemiah 8:10 says, "The joy of the Lord is your strength." Shortly before the Cross, Jesus prayed these words: "These things I speak in the world, that they may have My joy fulfilled in themselves" (John 17:13). You may protest and say that Jesus was talking about our future joy in heaven. Yet Jesus went on to say, "I do not pray that You should take them out of the world, but that You should keep them from the evil one" (v. 15). It is "the evil one" who hinders our joy in the Christian life. Joy is the birthright and privilege of every Christian.

Once I was preaching the truths of spiritual freedom in an east Tennessee church. I was focusing on freedom from the "spirit of heaviness" or depression. After teaching I led the people through a prayer, repudiating the spirit of heaviness and releasing the fruit of the Spirit, which includes joy. I began reading Isaiah 61:3: "[I will] give them . . . the garment of praise for the spirit of heaviness." I then turned to Romans 14:17: "For the kingdom of God is not eating and drinking, but righteousness and peace and joy in the Holy Spirit." Suddenly a young woman, normally extremely shy, began to laugh, weep, and shout, "Praise the Lord, I am free, I'm free!" The truth of her freedom exploded in joy and poured out of her. Joy is the birthright of every Christian.

Freedom in Christ Is Evident to the Unchurched

Then they said among the nations, "The Lord has done great things for them." The Lord has done great things for us, and we are glad (vv. 2, 3).

The joy of ended captivity is convincing evidence to the unreached around us. Seeing people delivered who have been in bondage is persuasive proof for witnessing. Christians who cannot handle the vicissitudes of life faithfully and joyfully have no effective witness for Christ. Yet when the unreached see the believer coping with anger, bitterness, pride, depression, and other problems in a victorious manner, then the message of Christ gets through. You see, Friend, being a witness means that your lifestyle is a part of the evidence.

A young-married woman began to experience real freedom in Christ from the assaults of depression by Satan. Though her problems and pressures were unchanged, her perspective changed as she began to see herself in Christ. Soon her children and husband came to Christ. Since that time others in her family have come to the Lord. When our lives are lived in Christ, then it is evident to the unchurched.

Freedom in Christ Releases the Flow of Revival

Bring back our captivity, O Lord, as the streams in the South (v. 4). Not long ago I was in Israel and we were scheduled to travel into normally dry southern Israel. Our Masada trip was postponed a day because of rains in Jerusalem. Southern Israel by the Dead Sea is the lowest point on the earth, so rains in upper Israel fill the stream beds in the south. These flowing streams give life to the land.

What a beautiful picture of revival! When believers are set free from the bondage of captivity, it releases the flow of the life of God into the church. The dry places are where demons live, according to Luke 11:24. When revival comes, God's "enemies are scattered" (Psalm 68:1). Real revival cannot come until the church knows her identity in Christ and begins to walk in the heritage of freedom.

Spiritual warfare is not destruction to revival; it is an impetus to revival. When believers experience the liberating power of the truth of the good news of Christ, then the power of God is released through them. Only when the church is released from carnal captivity will the Spirit of God be released in heaven-sent revival.

Freedom in Christ Inspires Evangelism

Those who sow in tears shall reap in joy. He who continually goes forth weeping, bearing seed for sowing, shall doubtless come again with rejoicing, bringing his sheaves with him (vv. 5, 6). These familiar verses are usually preached alone, calling the church to passionate soulwinning. Yet, the sowing and reaping can only take place if the people have come home from spiritual bondage to the "promised land" of the Spirit-filled life.

How futile to call on people to sow and reap in the rocky and infertile soil of a spiritual wasteland. It is in the fertile land of the will of God that believers find the Bible to be a rich bag of precious life-giving seeds. Only when one is free can he or she effectively sow in tears and reap in joy.

God promises revival and a harvest to those who come home from bondage. Believers can experience freedom that leads to a new effectiveness in their witness.

21

CLEANSING THE ROAD TO FREEDOM

Now I, Paul, myself am pleading with you by the meekness and gentleness of Christ—who in presence am lowly among you, but being absent am bold toward you. But I beg you that when I am present I may not be bold with that confidence by which I intend to be bold against some, who think of us as if we walked according to the flesh.

For though we walk in the flesh, we do not war according to the flesh. For the weapons of our warfare are not carnal but mighty in God for pulling down strongholds, casting down arguments and every high thing that exalts itself against the knowledge of God, bringing every thought into captivity to the obedience of Christ (2 Corinthians 10:1-5).

Though believers can never be totally overtaken by Satan and his demons, the sad reality is that many are harassed constantly by wicked forces. Whenever the flesh is in control of a Christian's life, demons are given a place in the believer's mind. This place is usually an unconfessed sin, an unbroken bad habit (obsession), or a wrong attitude. Simply stated, the believer has embraced a lie. Verse 5 says, "Casting down arguments and every high thing that exalts itself against the knowledge of God." The battle rages in the mind of the Christian. Sometimes wrong ideas, bad attitudes, false assumptions, wrong tradition, and lies harbor demons.

The Definition of a Stronghold

A stronghold is a fortress of wrong thinking that can harbor a demonic spirit or influence. The demonic influence can launch attacks from the house that our wrong thinking has erected for Satan. We erect houses for demons to live in. Indeed, we put the gun in the Enemy's hand for him to shoot us.

Habits and addictions are often demonically infested strongholds. This is not demon possession but demon infestation. Christians can be oppressed, depressed, tempted, harassed, and buffeted, but they cannot be possessed.

The Description of a Stronghold

Ephesians 4:17-32 describes the walk or manner of life of the believer. Paul takes sinful acts and traces them to their psychological origin. Verses 22, 23, and 27 indicate that we give place to the devil in our minds. All of Satan's strongholds begin in an unkempt thought life. A person allows the mind to dwell on wrong thoughts. Every habit is like a scratch in a record. Every time the circumstances come around, one hits the rut. This pattern can be broken only by replacing the record with a new one.

Ephesians 4 mentions the following sins that give Satan a stronghold in one's life:

Intellectual foolishness. "This I say, therefore, and testify in the Lord, that you should no longer walk as the rest of the Gentiles walk, in the futility of their mind, having their understanding darkened, being alienated from the life of God, because of the ignorance that is in them, because of the blindness of their heart" (vv. 17, 18).

Greed for impurity. "Having their understanding darkened, being alienated from the life of God, because of the ignorance that is in them, because of the blindness of their heart; who, being past feeling, have given themselves over to lewdness, to work all uncleanness with greediness. But you have not so learned Christ, if indeed you have heard Him and have been taught by Him, as the truth is in Jesus: that you put off, concerning your former conduct, the old man which grows corrupt according to the deceitful lusts" (vv. 18-22).

Dishonesty. "Therefore, putting away lying, 'Let each one of you speak truth with his neighbor,' for we are members of one another" (v. 25).

Uncontrolled anger. "Be angry, and do not sin" (v. 26).

An unforgiving spirit. "Do not let the sun go down on your wrath" (v. 26).

Theft. "Let him who stole steal no longer" (v. 28).

Slothfulness. "But rather let him labor, working with his hands what is good, that he may have something to give him who has need" (v. 28).

These sins affirm the maxim, "The idle mind is the devil's workshop." Satan has free reign because of so much false thinking being taught and practiced. For example, secular humanism makes man an accident of evolution. Hedonism makes itself so appealing it has man begging for more and more perversion. Violence, and the threat of it, is overwhelming us. Stealing and sloth are twin evils that seem to be taken for granted.

Take a child and give him all he wants. When the child reaches the teen years, let him play music with an animalistic beat and satanic, vulgar, drug-oriented, sex-oriented lyrics. Give him plenty of free time and bankroll the activities. Satan will soon have a prisoner. Young people will lie and steal from hardworking parents to support drug habits.

Take a man and feed his mind on immoral movies and pornographic magazines. Soon he will be enslaved. He will have an affair and destroy his home. He may become a child beater. Most child beaters are addicted to pornographic materials.

Take a woman and let her idle away her time watching vulgar soap operas—those ridiculous, immoral plots that glorify adultery, promote divorce, and set a substandard for living. Soon this person will be addicted—hooked on television like a drug addict to heroin. God deliver us from a generation that is more involved with the lives of imaginary characters in a television program than they are of the woes of human beings around them in real-life situations. They need Christ! Sin is habit-forming.

Stealing begins with the small things and grows. Lying begins with the "white lie" and goes to the "black one." Unforgiveness leads to hatred. Lust leads to immorality. Satan builds a fortress—a pattern of thinking that only the blood of Jesus can bring down.

The Danger of Strongholds

Strongholds are dangerous to Christians. Undetected and unremoved, they will eventually destroy you. You cannot have détente with the devil. There can be no peaceful coexistence with the prince of darkness. There can be no treaty with Satan. He will destroy you. Scripture warns us, "Be sober, be vigilant; because your adversary the devil walks about like a roaring lion, seeking whom he may devour" (1 Peter 5:8).

Evil attitudes may grow into evil acts that become habits. Satan inhabits our habits! They are his destructive strongholds.

With Peter, it was pride that brought him down. With Judas, it was greed. With Ananias and Sapphira, it was lying. With Demas, it was lust. Satan will destroy you if you give him a place in your life.

The Destruction of Strongholds

Our weapons are "mighty in God for pulling down strongholds" (2 Corinthians 10:4). These strongholds are in the territory of your soul, or mind. Thus the weapons of God pull down imaginations and thoughts that are erected against the knowledge of God (v. 5).

These weapons are God's Word and prayer applying the victory of Christ to Satan. Revelation 12:11 describes the use of these weapons: "And they overcame him [Satan] by the blood of the Lamb and by the word of their testimony, and they did not love their lives to the death." We see the atoning blood, the witness of the armed believer, and the life abandoned to the will of Jesus. Satan trembles before the believer with God's weapons.

Here are eight steps to the removal of a stronghold.

1. Be sure you are saved.

2. Realize that only God can remove a stronghold.

3. Identify the stronghold.

4. Confess all sins related to the stronghold.

5. Thank God for forgiveness.

6. Visualize the destruction.

7. Ask God to free you from the negative demonic force associated with strongholds.

8. Make restitution.

After following these steps, one must possess the reclaimed territory. Reckon the flesh dead to that area and claim God's fullness. Be finished with the sins that enslaved you. Memorize Scripture to reinforce the victory.

In the Old Testament the Jews were told to drive out the enemy and possess Canaan. Abundant life awaits those of us who will drive out the Enemy and possess the land of our souls. The fortress of Jericho fell down before the people of God. Satan's fortress will crumble before us if we wield our weapons in the Spirit.

22

SLAMMING THE DOOR IN THE ENEMY'S FACE

Nor give place to the devil (Ephesians 4:27).

The Lord Jesus Christ himself is the victory. He has left us in a world where the Enemy is still on the loose. Satan is still a destructive force, but he is also a defeated foe. The church has been founded and commissioned to attack the gates of Satan's realm and enforce the victory of Calvary.

Many are coming to understand the reality of John 8:32: "You shall know the truth, and the truth shall make you free." How can the believer live and walk in freedom? How can we slam the door in the face of the Enemy when he knocks?

Understand The Enemy's Approach

The strategy of Satan is to steal the seed of God's Word. Notice his thievery from the hearts of people who are hearing God's Word: "When anyone hears the word of the kingdom, and does not understand it, then the wicked one comes and snatches away what was sown in his heart. This is he who received seed by the wayside" (Matthew 13:19).

Satan desires to fill the church with lost people. Notice that Satan works in the same field in which we labor. "The field is the world, the good seeds are the sons of the kingdom, but the tares are the sons of the wicked one. The enemy who sowed them is the devil, the harvest is the end of the age, and the reapers are the angels" (vv. 38, 39).

Satan opposes the truth. He hates the truth. John said: "You are of your father the devil, and the desires of your father you want to do. He was a murderer from the beginning, and does not stand in the truth, because there is no truth in him. When he speaks a lie, he speaks from his own resources, for he is a liar and the father of it" (John 8:44).

Satan motivates people to sin. Notice three passages that reveal Satan's operation:

- "And supper being ended, the devil having already put it into the heart of Judas Iscariot, Simon's son, to betray Him . . ." (John 13:2).

- "Peter said, 'Ananias, why has Satan filled your heart to lie to the Holy Spirit and keep back part of the price of the land for yourself?'" (Acts 5:3).

- "In which you once walked according to the course of this world, according to the prince of the power of the air, the spirit who now works in the sons of disobedience" (Ephesians 2:2).

Satan desires to devour your life. Simon Peter portrays the Enemy as a vicious lion: "Be sober, be vigilant; because your adversary the devil walks about like a roaring lion, seeking whom he may devour" (1 Peter 5:8).

Satan twists the Scriptures. In tempting Jesus, Satan quoted Scripture: "'He shall give His angels charge over you,' and, 'In their hands they shall bear you up, lest you dash your foot against a stone'" (Matthew 4:6).

Satan has cunning plans. Paul reminds us of Satan's devious schemes: "Lest Satan should take advantage of us; for we are not ignorant of his devices" (2 Corinthians 2:11).

Satan comes in deceptive disguises. He can come to us as a minister or a dedicated believer. "And no wonder! For Satan himself transforms himself into an angel of light" (2 Corinthians 11:14).

Satan tempts in areas of weakness. Notice the Bible's warning about sexual needs in marriage:

Now concerning the things of which you wrote to me: It is good for a man not to touch a woman. Nevertheless, because of sexual immorality, let each man have his own wife, and let each woman have her own husband. Let the husband render to his wife the affection due her, and likewise also the wife to her husband. The wife does not have authority over her own body, but the husband does. And likewise the husband does not have authority over his own body, but the wife does. Do not deprive one another except with consent for a time, that you may give yourselves to fasting and prayer; and come together again so that Satan does not tempt you because of your lack of self-control (1 Corinthians 7:1-5).

Satan desires to set your focus on the interests of this world rather than on God. Satan will often speak through some well-meaning friend. Satan used Simon Peter to attack Jesus:

From that time Jesus began to show to His disciples that He must go to Jerusalem, and suffer many` things from the elders and chief priests and scribes, and be killed, and be raised the third day.

Then Peter took Him aside and began to rebuke Him, saying, "Far be it from You, Lord; this shall not happen to You!"

But He turned and said to Peter, "Get behind Me, Satan! You are an offense to Me, for you are not mindful of the things of God, but the things of men."

Then Jesus said to His disciples, "If anyone desires to come after Me, let him deny himself, and take up his cross, and follow Me. For whoever desires to save his life will lose it, but whoever loses his life for My sake will find it. For what profit is it to a man if he gains the whole world, and loses his own soul? Or what will a man give in exchange for his soul? (Matthew 16:21-26).

Satan energizes the lost world. Paul described the bondage of the lost: "In which you once walked according to the course of this world, according to the prince of the power of the air, the spirit who now works in the sons of disobedience" (Ephesians 2:2).

The Decision to Live in Victory

Know, first, that spiritual warfare is no quick fix. The ministry of spiritual warfare must be married to a commitment to a crucified and disciplined life. It must include daily repentance and renewal of the thought life. It must encompass recognition of God's work in conforming you to the image of Christ.

Spiritual warfare must remain focused on Christ, His victory, and His mission. Most spiritual warfare is done by individual believers allowing the Holy Spirit to control the mind and the flesh.

In looking at the words *war* and *warfare* in the New Testament, we discover that the devil is hardly mentioned.

For victorious warfare, we must cast down mental bondage. "Casting down arguments and every high thing that exalts itself against the knowledge of God" (2 Corinthians 10:5). We must decide once and for all to take our thought lives captive.

For victorious warfare, we must stay sound in the faith. "This charge I commit to you, son Timothy, according to the prophecies previously made concerning you, that by them you may wage the good warfare" (1 Timothy 1:18).

For victorious warfare, we are warned not to become cluttered by the world's entanglements. "No one engaged in warfare entangles himself with the affairs of this life, that he may please him who enlisted him as a soldier" (2 Timothy 2:4).

For victorious warfare, we are told to harness the lusts of the flesh. "Where do wars and fights come from among you? Do they not come from your desires for pleasure that war in your members?" (James 4:1). You can live in freedom and victory the moment you decide to take God at His word.

This freedom will be a walk, a journey—not a quick fix. It will radically alter your life.

Slamming the Door in the Enemy's Face

Demon spirits have absolutely no power to bring about destruction unless they can find an open door into a person's mind. If we as believers ignore the Holy Spirit's pleading and allow sin, temptation, wrong attitudes, and past hurts to go unconfessed, unchallenged, and unchanged, then we leave a gaping hole through which the Enemy will seek to undo us. Most spiritual destruction is avoidable if we will reverently listen to the pleading of the Spirit and obey His warning to us.

Never try to shift the blame for your responsibilities to the Enemy. That makes you a liar and opens another door to the Enemy. Adam blamed Eve and Eve blamed the devil, but ultimately they were each responsible for the choice to sin. I don't care if a million demons have been assigned to destroy you, they cannot gain entry or destroy you without your giving them a place of entry.

Recognize that a surprise attack from the Enemy often comes just before a major breakthrough in your life or church. In Mark 4:35-41 a surprise mega-storm arose against Jesus and the disciples just before they were about to release the demoniac at Gadara (5:1-20). After Jesus rebuked the winds, there was a "megacalm." Whenever the Enemy strikes an unexpected blow, remember that God is about to bring a major breakthrough. Stand firm during a crisis.

Never try to fight the Enemy with fleshly weapons. The flesh is no match for the enemies in the spiritual realm. Regardless of how good it looks, or how loud it roars, it is no match for spiritual enemies.

Put on the armor of God and stand dressed up in Christ as your sure defense. Take the weapon of God's Word, prayer, praise, the blood of Jesus, and the name of Jesus. Assume your position and authority in Christ's throne and believe that the Enemy is under your feet.

Learn to live behind the hedge of God's protection. Isaiah 5:1-7 presents the awful picture of a nation that had lost its hedge of God's protection and became prey to the enemy.

In Israel a vineyard sometimes had three hedges: a stone wall, a hedge of thorns, and at harvest time a wall of fire. God can put hedges around nations, families, individuals, and churches. In Job's case God removed the hedge and allowed the Enemy to attack Job to prove that Satan was a liar. If you are right with God and under attack, God is proving Satan a liar concerning you!

You live behind God's hedge when you live under God's authority. You build the hedge by prayer. Individually the hedge is God's armor. For the church and nation, God uses His anointed ones. God said, "So I sought for a man among them who would make a wall, and stand in the gap before Me on behalf of the land, that I should not destroy it; but I found no one" (Ezekiel 22:30). Remember Sodom; had 10 righteous people been found, the city would have been spared.

I am convinced that walls of protection are also available to us today.

The first wall is Jesus Christ, a wall of stone. "The stone which the builders rejected has become the chief cornerstone" (Luke 20:17).

The second wall is God's angelic protection, a hedge of thorns. "The angel of the Lord encamps all around those who fear Him, and delivers them" (Psalm 34:7).

The third wall is like a wall of fire around you: it is salvation and praise. "You shall call your walls Salvation, and your gates Praise" (Isaiah 60:18).

23

PUTTING THE ENEMY TO FLIGHT

Where do wars and fights come from among you? Do they not come from your desires for pleasure that war in your members? You lust and do not have. You murder and covet and cannot obtain. You fight and war. Yet you do not have because you do not ask. You ask and do not receive, because you ask amiss, that you may spend it on your pleasures. Adulterers and adulteresses! Do you not know that friendship with the world is enmity with God? Whoever therefore wants to be a friend of the world makes himself an enemy of God. Or do you think that the Scripture says in vain, "The Spirit who dwells in us yearns jealously"?

But He gives more grace. Therefore He says: "God resists the proud, but gives grace to the humble."

Therefore submit to God. Resist the devil and he will flee from you (James 4:1-7).

Satan has been stripped of authority in the life of every believer. Satan and his demonic forces fear the authority of the Word of God through Christ. James 2:19 says, "Even the demons believe—and tremble!" A decisive battle was waged and won at the Cross and the empty tomb, stripping Satan and his hosts of authority. Colossians 2:15 declares that Jesus "disarmed principalities and powers [of their authority]."

When Jesus came to the world, it was an occupied armed camp of Satan. The forces of evil recognized Him (Mark 1:23-25). In Mark 5, evil forces encamped in a man. Enough demons controlled him to fill 2,000 swine. But notice that these forces could not move without the permission of Jesus. Jesus defeated Satan and broke his authority at every point.

Satan could not receive Jesus. He could not get Jesus to yield to temptation. Death could not hold Jesus. Satan used every weapon and found them broken under the feet of Christ. The glorious truth is that you and I can enforce that victory. We can put the Enemy to flight. We can see Satan in rapid retreat. Here are the simple steps to victory.

The Requirement of Submission

God resists the proud, but gives grace to the humble (James 4:6). Before a believer can effectively put Satan to flight, he must be under authority himself. God resists the proud. The word *proud* describes a self-sufficient person who runs his own life. The word *resist* means "to arrange an army against." God has placed an army against the self-sufficient.

The key word in verse 7 is *submit.* It is a military word which means "to place under orders." A believer has authority over Satan by living under the authority of Christ. A rebellious, sinning Christian cannot put Satan to flight. The Christian who lives under God-given authority can put the Enemy to flight. Believers must learn to live under authority. The Word of God sets forth God's pattern of authority.

Christians live under the authority of Christ. We also live under the authority of human government (1 Peter 2:13-15). The wife is to live under the authority of her husband (Ephesians 5:22-24). Children are to live under the authority of parents (Ephesians 6:1-3). This is for protection and power.

All human authority is delegated but is invalid if it violates the will of God. "We ought to obey God rather than men" (Acts 5:29).

We are told that if we are to defeat Satan, we must be under orders. Jesus lived under the will of the Father in His earthly sojourn. This was the secret of His power. He lived under authority. "He humbled Himself and became obedient to the point of death" (Philippians 2:8). This was the prelude to victory. This was the path to authority. After His submission came His exaltation. Verse 10 declares that every realm is now under His authority—the spiritual realm, the natural realm, and the demonic realm. Before we can stand in authority, we must submit ourselves to God completely.

The Resistance of Satan

Therefore submit to God. Resist the devil and he will flee from you (James 4:7). Once we are under authority, we can stand in Christ's authority. Ephesians 1 and 2 declares this truth.

- *Ephesians 1:19-23* declares the authority of the risen, ascended, and enthroned Christ. We must recognize that we have no authority over Satan in our own flesh and power. We are made lower than the angels. But in Christ we have been given His authority over Satan.

- *Ephesians 2:1-6* declares that we are now fully identified with Christ in crucifixion, resurrection, ascension, and in being enthroned. Thus, we now share His authority. We are now in Him, elevated above the angelic realm. (See chapter 9 of this book.)

We are to *resist* Satan. This word in verse 7 is not the same as the word in verse 6. The word in verse 7 implies to "stand alone." It pictures the believer and God against Satan. We stand without human help.

We must learn that we cannot hide from Satan. We cannot run away from Satan. We cannot outrun him, and we cannot get away from him on this planet.

How, then, do we resist Satan?

- Be sure you are living, under authority, an obedient and clean life.

- Take your stand against Satan in the authority of Christ.

- Stand steadfast in faith, believing God for the victory.

- Verbally attack Satan with the Word of God and the work of Christ.

- Give no place to Satan; give up no ground whatever.

- Demand in the authority of Christ that he leave.

- Give thanks and praise to God and watch the devil run.

"Thanks be to God who always leads us in triumph in Christ" (2 Corinthians 2:14). The battle is ours in Christ. We must stand against Satan at his every attack. These are four great battlegrounds for all of us today:

- *Satan attacks through the occult.* This includes New Age, witchcraft, horoscope, Ouija boards, tarot cards, palm readers, hard rock music, and drugs.

- *Satan hates and attacks the home.* This is the scene of his greatest attack.

- *Satan attacks and troubles the mind.* A religious secular humanism is now the sanctioned belief of the state. False humanistic philosophy destroys the moral fiber of those who believe them.

- *Satan attacks religion by using it.* He is transformed into an angel of light. False teachers arise in the last days. We must resist the Enemy, and when we do, he must flee!

24

LIVING IN TRIUMPH

But one of the elders said to me, "Do not weep. Behold, the Lion of the tribe of Judah, the Root of David, has prevailed to open the scroll and to loose its seven seals."

And I looked, and behold, in the midst of the throne and of the four living creatures, and in the midst of the elders, stood a Lamb as though it had been slain, having seven horns and seven eyes, which are the seven Spirits of God sent out into all the earth (Revelation 5:5, 6).

> Now I saw heaven opened, and behold, a white horse. And He who sat on him was called Faithful and True, and in righteousness He judges and makes war (19:11).

I recently received a heartbreaking but anonymous letter from a member of our television family. This dear lady cataloged a life of abuse that rivals the abuse endured by the woman in Alice Walker's *Color Purple.* She had been hated by her father, beaten with pokers, molested by brothers and an uncle, cursed and abused by her present husband. When she sought help from her religion, she was told she could not take Communion and that she was going to hell because she was married before she wed her present husband. She writes: "All I do is hate myself for my sins. . . . I could end my life, but I listened to you last Sunday, I cried and was happy. Then my husband cursed me out. . . . I respect your TV sermons. I feel as if I am at church. My church disowns me because I believe God can heal and I don't believe all other churches are going to hell. Does God hate me—is that why I have so much grief?"

For some people, life on earth may always seem to hold heartache and grief. Yet, we can have a new perspective when we understand who Christ is and what He is doing and will do for His children. Victory belongs to the believer now. One day, at His coming, all of hell's forces will be brought to judgment. Let us conclude this study with this challenge to live in triumph.

When John wrote Revelation, the whole world was under the sway of a cruel Roman Empire. These were the days of Nero and Caligula, madmen who made life miserable for those who believed in God and confessed Jesus as Lord.

For his part, John the apostle was exiled to the barren island called Patmos. He was there simply because of his commitment to God's Word and his testimony about Jesus. God did not hate John, nor does He hate the dear lady who wrote to me. He allows us to live in this sin-cursed world so that we will learn utter dependence on Him.

As you read through Revelation, you may notice a word that is usually unnoticed but often repeated. That word is "Behold. . . ." Like a narrow window gazing out of a dungeon of despair, the troubled church in a graphic world is called to look beyond its present distress to a victory already achieved!

The word *behold* is translated from a Greek imperative, meaning "see." The structure of this verb means "to arouse attention"; "to introduce something new, extraordinary, and important"; and it was "a call to consideration and contemplation." It was as if God was saying, "Look, look . . . give Me your attention! Here is something new and exciting, something extraordinary and important for you to see." God wants us to see beyond our circumstances, so that we can live in victory. I have selected five occasions where God calls His people to "behold."

Behold a Risen Savior

I am He who lives, and was dead, and behold, I am alive forevermore. Amen. And I have the keys of Hades and of Death (Revelation 1:18).

To John, alone on Patmos, Jesus said, "Look, John, I am alive." Writers have said that the actress Rita Hayworth would often call the fire department with a false alarm just to have someone to talk to. Loneliness is a terrible feeling. In this scripture Jesus is saying to John and to all of us, "If you will only look, you will see that I am alive and I am here!"

In the dark valleys of life, when the lion of hell roars his loudest, you can confess, "Though I walk through the valley of the shadow of death . . . You are with me" (Psalm 23:4).

Behold an Open Heaven

After these things I looked, and behold, a door standing open in heaven. And the first voice which I heard was like a trumpet speaking with me, saying, "Come up here, and I will show you things which must take place after this" (Revelation 4:1).

We live in a world of closed doors. Disappointments come incessantly, like waves of the ocean. How many have failed to get the job, the scholarship, the mate, the hope? How many have experienced broken dreams, broken engagements, broken promises, broken health, and broken hearts? How often have you looked around and viewed nothing but locked doors?

John knew about closed doors as he gazed from his rocky prison across the sea to where friends and family waited. There was no rapture to rescue him. No ship sailed up to take him home. Yet he heard a voice, indeed the voice of the ages, cry, "Look, look!" and when John looked, he saw heaven opened.

Do you understand that Jesus has gained for us an audience in heaven? When every door on earth seems closed, heaven's gate stands forever open for the praying Christian.

Behold a Throne Set

Immediately I was in the Spirit; and behold, a throne set in heaven, and One sat on the throne (Revelation 4:2). The word *throne* speaks of authority and sovereignty. When you view that throne, you see that it was "set." This means literally it was "laid down" in the past with continuing results. This throne has been established and will forever be in place. Upon this throne is the One who shines like a diamond.

Around the throne is the rainbow of faithfulness. Out of this throne are the evidences of power and authority.

This is the throne we will share in victory with our Lord. When it seems that life offers no hope, when all the foundations of life crumble, when there are no answers, when everything seems to be shaken— remember: there is a "throne set in heaven" that shall never be moved!

Behold a Prevailing Lord

But one of the elders said to me, "Do not weep. Behold, the Lion of the tribe of Judah, the Root of David, has prevailed to open the scroll and to loose its seven seals." And I looked, and behold, in the midst of the throne and of the four living creatures, and in the midst of the elders, stood a Lamb as though it had been slain, having seven horns and seven eyes, which are the seven Spirits of God sent out into all the earth (Revelation 5:5, 6).

In this scene the indictment has been handed down against all humanity. The book is written and humanity is guilty. This sin, this awful guilt, cannot be undone by the intelligence or efforts of humanity. Neither education nor sophistication nor human ingenuity can crack the curse on this world. There is nothing that humankind can do to break the bondages of the fall. Yet, listen to the angel cry, "Look, look . . . can't you see that the Lion of Judah has prevailed?" The word *prevailed* translates an aorist verb—*enikesen*—from *nikao*, which means "to conquer forever." The verb *open* is also an aorist infinitive which means "forever opened." You see, the book is opened and the curse is broken forever. Jesus has prevailed over all that is against us forever!

When we look beyond the crown of the Lion, we see the cross of the Lamb. We see the mastery of the Lion and the mystery of the Lamb. This Lamb bore the scars of violent death. Calvary was where the bloody battle was fought and won.

Some time ago my wife brought home some old *Life* magazines from the '60s. I was intrigued by an issue that portrayed 242 men who had died in one week in Vietnam. Their pictures, plus the last letters and vignettes from their lives were printed. In a letter written a day before his death, one young man wrote, "I see death coming up the hill." Somehow you could feel the terror in that sentence. As the walls of communism and totalitarianism crumble, we now know that our men did not die in vain.

Death and hell came up the hill of Calvary and did its worst to Jesus, yet He prevailed on the cross and is alive forevermore!

Behold a Coming Lord

Now I saw heaven opened, and behold, a white horse. And He who sat on him was called Faithful and True, and in righteousness He judges and makes war (Revelation 19:11).

"Behold, I am coming quickly! Blessed is he who keeps the words of the prophecy of this book" (22:7).

"And behold, I am coming quickly, and My reward is with Me, to give to every one according to his work" (22:12).

He who testifies to these things says, "Surely I am coming quickly" (22:20).

All of these verses cry, "Look, look, Jesus is coming." History has a hope. The One who prevailed as the Alpha will come as the Omega. He who was the "Genesis" will also be the "Revelation." This life is a prelude to a better life. Because Jesus has prevailed, so shall every child of God. "Even so, come, Lord Jesus!" (Revelation 22:20).